MESSAGES FROM THE
Higher Self

NATALIE WALSTEIN

divine flow
PUBLISHING CO.
Honolulu, Hawaii

Copyright © 2024 by Natalie Walstein

Cover design: Jennifer Ann Birge

Published in the United States by Divine Flow Publishing Co.
Honolulu, Hawaii • www.divineflow.co

All rights reserved. This book or any portion thereof may not be reproduced or used in any manner whatsoever without the express written permission of the publisher except for the use of brief quotations in a book review.

The author of this book does not dispense medical advice or prescribe the use of any technique as a form of treatment for physical, emotional, or medical problems without the advice of a physician, either directly or indirectly. The intent of the author is only to offer information of a general nature to help you in your quest for emotional, physical, and spiritual well-being. In the event you use any of the information in this book for yourself, the author and the publisher assume no responsibility for your actions.

Hardcover Print ISBN: 979-8-9916794-1-1

Paperback Print ISBN: 979-8-9916794-2-8

eBook ISBN: 979-8-9916794-0-4

Publisher's Cataloging-in-Publication Data
Names: Walstein, Natalie.
Title: Messages from the higher self / Natalie Walstein.
Description: Honolulu, HI : Divine Flow Publishing, 2024. | Summary: Presents a way of connecting with the Higher Self, the wise and ancient aspect of the Soul that governs a person's life plan and decides on the lessons meant to be learned in each lifetime. Through hypnosis, one can ask questions of the Higher Self and receive deep, immersive messages.
Identifiers: LCCN 2024922067 | ISBN 9798991679411 (hardback) | ISBN 9798991679404 (ebook)
Subjects: LCSH: Channeling (Spiritualism). | Hypnotism. | Guides (Spiritualism). | Energy medicine. | Metaphysics. | BISAC: BODY, MIND & SPIRIT / Angels & Spirit Guides. | BODY, MIND & SPIRIT / Channeling & Mediumship.
Classification: LCC BF1275.S55 .W35 2024 | DDC 133.9 W--dc23
LC record available at https://lccn.loc.gov/2024922067

To myself in a past life, who tried to tell the revelatory stories of spiritual awakening experiences around the campfire but wasn't believed or appreciated.

And to my Higher Self for helping us change that now!

TABLE OF CONTENTS

Prologue..I

Chapter 1: Introduction.....................................1

Chapter 2: My First Session............................15

Chapter 3: Awakening to Past Life Wisdom......71

Chapter 4: The Life Review & Pre-Planning Process......105

Chapter 5: Choosing to Embrace Chaos..........117

Chapter 6: Healing from Past Incarnations......127

Chapter 7: Parallel Lives on Other Planets......159

Chapter 8: Our Otherworldly Abilities............181

Chapter 9: Healing Goddess Energy................215

Chapter 10: Merging with Your Higher Self......245

Additional Resources......................................276

Acknowledgments...278

About the Author..279

PROLOGUE

I first remember dreaming about things before they happen when I was 18 years old. This was the beginning of my journey of connecting with the concept of a Higher Self.

I had recently graduated from high school when I dreamed I was on a wondrous bike ride with two of my friends, Nik and Hayley. In the dream, all three of us had red bikes. We went for a joy ride from our neighborhood, through the grounds of our former high school nearby, into the woods along a stream, all the way to a string of lakes a few miles away.

It was a beautiful summer day that was nearly idyllic, made even better by the fact that we were celebrating our newfound freedom from school. It was the kind of day you wish you could live over and over again, but it was just a dream. I didn't even own a red bike.

A few weeks later, when Nik and Hayley showed up at my house with three red bikes they'd gathered from a garage sale, I didn't immediately make the connection to the dream. It wasn't until the three of us rode them all the way to the lake that it finally dawned on me that absolutely everything I was seeing that day—from the places we went to the people we had seen, the pictures we took, and the laughter we shared, to eventually stopping for ice cream on the way back home to our neighborhood—had already all happened before, in that exact order, in that magical dream only a few weeks before.

After taking a break from pedaling at the lake, I set down my red beach cruiser bike, the only one of the three that had *Good Vibrations* printed down the side. I walked to the edge of the water, and there I saw the beautiful sky reflected perfectly on the surface of the lake, like a scene from a painting. That's when I let the full realization wash over me that I had seen and experienced this entire adventure before. It was a surprising and unusual feeling of deja vu that lasted the whole afternoon.

I drank in the experience and tried to process what it meant. Since I didn't know, at 18 years old, what it meant to have a prophetic dream or what I was even meant to do with this newfound ability, I simply chalked it up to being one of the many unexplainable and unknowable mysteries of the universe. I waited to see if the reason behind it would ever come to light, but that magical first time I pre-dreamed my reality seemed for many years to be a special rare occurrence.

It wasn't until later, in my mid-20s, that I started realizing that I was dreaming about absolutely everything before it happened all the time. The feeling of deja vu had slowly begun to spread throughout my entire life, to the point where I was dreaming about everything I was going to experience a few weeks beforehand - not just the magical moments, but all of them. It was like living inside an echo.

This was super confusing and ethereal and something I just learned to get used to without knowing why it was happening or what exactly I was meant to do with it. When I told others what I was experiencing, they seemed just as baffled by it as I was. I began to accept it as a normal part of being the strange person that was me.

As I got older, this precognitive dreaming phenomenon continued to progress even further. It was in my early 30s, in particular, when the dreams started becoming a lot more detailed. It was at this point that I started to realize that I was not only dreaming about every single thing before it happened, but I was also the one planning for everything to happen.

Pre-Planning Our Lives

Imagine experiencing your life in a dream as if you are the main character in a movie. Then, imagine if you could zoom out and see the whole production team that is crafting the movie behind the scenes. What if you could also chat with them about the upcoming scenes, the props, and the people you would need to have on hand to give your very best performance? This is what began happening in my dreams.

In my dreams, I would sit across from what can only be described as one of my spirit guides, and we would have a whole conversation about what I could expect to happen next in my life. They explained everything I was going to experience, from the small details all the way to the big, life-altering events. Sometimes, I was given months of material all at once, and I'd wake up feeling overwhelmed, thinking, "Whoa! This is going to be intense. Here we gooo!"

Sometimes, I would even remember my response to hearing about my future. I'd occasionally complain or ask questions, and the guide sitting across from me would help me see the bigger picture of why these experiences were important for my soul growth. They would show me alternate paths I could take while explaining the pros and cons of each. The reasons they provided me with always comforted me and even made me feel excited about what was to come, even if it was going to be especially challenging.

Over time, this experience developed even further and became more of a collaborative effort where I was given a choice on which path to take. I began noticing I was not simply being shown what would happen next in my life by some magical outside force; I was one of the spirits who was dictating it as part of a planning committee for my own life.

My spirit guides would lay out the specific life lessons, astrological and world influences, and other soul contracts I would be working with, and then it was as if they were consulting me on the best way for my human self to learn the lessons. I would hear about the plans that were being made and weigh in on what I felt would be the most effective way to master what I most needed to learn.

The guides sometimes showed me an easy, intermediate, and difficult path and what I would learn or receive if I chose each path. At the end of the day, it was my decision how far I wanted to take things, but the hardest paths always gave the best outcomes and brought me closest to my true desires, which made them seem much more attractive.

I saw that I was the one planning out how to realize my dreams for my life, just as I was the one planning for myself to get sick, to have injuries, to be rejected, and have things not work out how my human self wanted them to. I was the one creating the experiences, setbacks, heartbreaks, roadblocks, and challenges for myself, as my spirit guides assisted me all along the way, all so that my soul could learn the lessons it needed to grow and receive more blessings and love. I was my own best friend and enemy, and I seemed to bring just as much joy and love to the process of planning the triumphs as I did the tribulations.

I'd remember saying to my guides, "No, I won't learn the lesson if we do it that way. Let's make it harder!" I could feel and hear myself *specifically* asking for particular challenges in my life, and I didn't seem to care about the discomfort I would have to go through. From that level of my soul, I only cared about the growth and enlightenment that would be waiting for me on the other side.

Sometimes, my guides would look at me and say, "Are you sure you want to do it *that way*?" And I would excitedly pump my fist like an excitable little kid drunk on power and reply, "Yes! Make it hurt!" The pain didn't phase me because I could see a wider perspective of how things would work out so much better for me in the long run if I withstood the discomfort, disappointment, and what seemed like inconvenient detours in my waking life. (Of course, upon remembering these exchanges as my human self, I always wished I would choose the "easy" option a little more often!)

In these next-level dreams, I also began remembering holding meetings with other people I know here on Earth… or people I would soon know. People who wanted to work with me would pop into my dream, and we would set up scenarios for our human selves to work together. Then, a few weeks later, their name would show up in my booking calendar for a coaching session. Old friends would ask if we could get together and help each other out with our soul lessons. Sometimes, deceased spirits who had already crossed over would ask me to help their adult children, with whom I would soon cross paths in my waking life. Once, I asked a soulmate from a past life to come on an overseas hypnosis retreat I was planning to go on so we could reconnect and support each other in this lifetime.

These are the kind of crazy things I was dreaming about every night, and they kept getting weirder and weirder. The dreams would happen. Weeks later, the planned events unfolded, and connections with these people were made in the 3D world. The old friend who connected with me in my dream would reach out to plan a lunch date. I'd meet the son or daughter of the spirit who had asked me to help that person, often by having a simple conversation. The man from my dream heard the call and showed up to the retreat after signing up "on a whim" the month before - without even knowing what the retreat even entailed! It seemed that not only was I planning my own life, but we were all in on planning our lives *together* from behind the veil as our lives were unfolding.

Meeting the Higher Self

So, there it is. My strange little secret that no one else I know of has seemed to share. I was being allowed to peek behind the veil not only to see my future but to realize that I was the one orchestrating it. Most notably, I realized I was co-creating my life from a perspective that was playful, light, excitable, and based on a strong hunger for growth and evolution. Was *this* my Higher Self?

"She" was me, but a version that was more pure, innocent, lively, and alight with unconditional love. She was less concerned with the pain, worry, and strife and more focused on furthering the ever-unfolding story of my evolution. Then, my human self would have to experience everything she planned for "us," with me not always remembering the dream until the moment was *just right* for it to reveal itself.

This ability wasn't a "Get Out of Jail Free" card for dealing with life's difficulties, however. I always had to fully learn the lessons through a totally embodied experience without any cheat codes or sneaky detours. I still had to live through it all as if I didn't have a clue because the dream memories were buried deep enough in my subconscious that I couldn't always conveniently access them when I wanted to.

In addition to the dreamtime meetings that would occur with my spirit guides, friends, and students, this ability also brought another surprising perk. I found I could occasionally view the life-planning sessions that other people had with their guides before they came into their lives. I could peer into why other people had made certain decisions about things such as physical attributes, soul connections, and life challenges. This would happen out of the blue without any effort or intention from me, and it always left me in awe. As far as I had known, I hadn't been born psychic, so gradually developing these abilities as I moved into adulthood was startling and often confusing.

Other times in my dreams, I saw all of our spirit selves gathering in a big stadium to plan world events together, such as wars and natural disasters. It was very similar to the conferences you may have seen in *Star Wars*, where the leaders were planning the fate of the universe, except we are all representing our human selves in spirit while planning our collective future together. Afterward, we would filter out into the hallways, discussing the information that had been presented and trading our thoughts and reactions. Ultimately, we accepted that the planned disasters were going to be necessary for our planet's evolution with grace, ease, and openness because we could see and appreciate the bigger picture they were leading us toward.

But why was this happening? Who was this spirit version of me who seemed so nonchalant about things? This "higher me" felt so playful, sweet, and fun-loving even as it planned my "inevitable self-destruction" (and resulting evolutionary growth). Even the incoming "unfortunate" developments that were soon to occur in the world seemed to be a cause for celebration because of the positive spiritual changes they would eventually bring to everyone involved.

I spent many years learning about spirit guides, angels, and ascended masters as I made my way into adulthood, but suddenly I began building a growing interest in the Higher Self - the higher consciousness of my own soul. Was that the version of me I was experiencing in my dreams? What was the nature of the Higher Self? How did this all work?

I seemed to be catching glimpses of my Higher Self in these extraordinary dreams I was having, but I wanted to know and understand more from an anchored human perspective about this incredible higher aspect of ourselves that is guiding everything behind the scenes.

Eventually, the universe led me to discover a way I could learn more about the ins and outs of the Higher Self and receive a more thorough divine explanation. It was through a modality that would allow me, and others I worked with, to channel our Higher Selves on demand.

Having a Conversation with the Higher Self

Whenever I had precognitive dreams and visions, it was always unexpected. I didn't seem to have any control over when they would come or how deep they would go. It was not like lucid dreaming, where you can seemingly call forth the people and experiences you want at any time. It felt like my spirit guides were collecting me to have the experience they wanted to show me on *their* timeline, and I did not have a conscious awareness of it happening every night.

When I discovered hypnosis, it became a turning point where I was able to have more power in calling forth opportunities and experiences that would bring me closer to understanding the Higher Self. In a state of hypnosis, you can move into a deeper brainwave state called "theta," which bypasses the thinking mind and overrides the ego. In this state, you can tap into the infinite memory bank of your subconscious mind without getting so stuck in the density of the here and now. You can view dream visions and past lives firsthand as if you are right there in the moment. You can channel your Higher Self without the use of psychedelic drugs or the need to be psychic.

I had already read many books about the discoveries of hypnotists working in the realm between lifetimes when I was guided to read a book by the late Dolores Cannon called *Between Death and Life*. It is filled with transcripts from sessions with people who were induced into a deep state of hypnosis and then interviewed about the nature of the soul and the universe as they answered questions from the perspective of their Higher Selves. It's the kind of book that completely shifts your reality. It's the kind that you can't put down, and you find yourself wanting to read straight through to the very end all in one sitting because it explains so many things you have always wondered about the meaning of life.

When I got to the end, the book disclosed where you can go to get a hypnosis session and channel these answers for yourself. I was astonished this was even an option! I couldn't imagine what kind of incredible insights would come through for me if I was already having these intense precognitive and pre-planning dreams. Needless to say, I booked a hypnosis session right away, and I had a very unexpected and life-changing experience that triggered me to eventually decide to become a hypnotist myself.

Working with Dolores Cannon's *Quantum Healing Hypnosis Technique* (often referred to more simply as QHHT®) first for myself and then later with a small group of clients as a trained practitioner myself, I was finally able to get the answers to the questions that had been percolating for me about the nature of the Higher Self... and so much more. I was able to have direct conversations with others' Higher Selves and ask them specific questions about why certain life events were planned and how the planning process even works in the spirit world.

Through this magical modality, I learned about past lives and how the feelings and events from those other places and times intermingle with our current existence in this life. I learned how our fears, worries, insecurities, illnesses, and ailments are often rooted in something that happened to us in another time and place. I learned how we are simply part of a worldwide play, showing up as characters with carefully planned parts and plots, with a splash of free will and chaos added to the mix for "fun", and we are indeed writing our own stories from both this level and a higher level simultaneously every day.

What to Expect in this Book

This book represents a deep dive into the subject of our Higher Self and how it is guiding us and preparing us for bigger and better things and higher levels of wisdom and knowledge, all day, every day, all the time, in every moment. You will read the real experiences of real people who have connected with their Higher Selves as they channel the answers to their own life questions, receiving incredible clarity and insight into common life challenges and the reasons behind why those challenges were chosen. You will also see that we are so much more than who we are in just this lifetime, with gifts and hidden talents we have brought forth from more mystical times.

Most importantly, you will read about how truly loved and supported you always are by unseen forces (including your own Higher Self), which your human mind has simply forgotten about, for the purpose of completely inserting yourself into the fully immersive experience of being you.

Going on this journey to seek out more information about the Higher Self has made me realize how incredibly safe and loved we are. How funny and cool life is! And how we have always been writing and editing our own story this whole time. It has changed my life and helped me trust that, even when everything seems to be falling apart all around us, it's actually all coming together perfectly.

I hope this book brings you inspiration to see your life from a higher perspective, to question, "Why would I have planned this life for myself?" and to become more trusting in the idea that your Higher Self knows exactly what it's doing for you, even if your human self doesn't ever seem to have a clue.

We pre-plan our lives. Not *everything*, but a lot of it. The major milestones, the messy bits, the fun bits, even the mistakes. We plan the dreams we're going to have. We plan the people we are going to meet, hurt, love, and collaborate with. We can even plan what will come through in psychic readings, aura photos, *and* hypnosis sessions ahead of time with the help of our spirit guides in our dreams.

Why do we plan our lives to be as hard and beautiful as they are, and how? What is the true nature of the Higher Self? Who are we really deep down? And what kind of things would your Higher Self say about the purpose behind the greatest challenges in your life if you could speak to them directly? Let's dive in and find out.

Chapter 1: Introduction

WHAT IS THE HIGHER SELF? The Higher Self is sometimes thought of as our "ideal self." The common perception is that it's some perfectly healed version of ourselves that always takes the higher path and acts as the bigger person. Some may even see it as the essence they aspire to become more like someday, without realizing that the Higher Self is already who we are and have always been.

I have found that the Higher Self resides on a deeper layer of our soul consciousness as it governs our lives from a level beyond human awareness. From behind the veil, it oversees your soul mission from every lifetime you've ever lived and keeps track of every memory of every experience you've ever had. It's a higher power that has existed long before your human self, and it will continue to exist long after this lifetime has ended. It contains the totality of your soul's experience–your cumulative energy–and the culmination of everything you've ever learned.

In essence, you *are* your Higher Self. You just forgot, and forgetting is the point. The metaphorical blinders you have on make it so you can only see what's right in front of you in this current lifetime. This way, you can focus on having the specific life experiences your soul desires to have without any irrelevant details or distractions getting in the way. Meanwhile, your Higher Self acts as the storehouse for all your soul's memories since the beginning of time, like your own personal recordkeeper. It remembers everything you truly are and everything you have ever been in all your incarnations on Earth (or elsewhere).

Along with your spirit team of teachers, guides, angels, and Ascended Masters, your Higher Self makes a plan for your life based on your past soul experiences and any areas of study you wish to master going forward. This plan can continue to change and evolve as you do, and there is always the element of free will. While life may feel chaotic and confusing at times, we can trust that there is always a bigger strategy running through our storylines.

It may be helpful to think of your human self as a video game character and your Higher Self as the one playing the game. The Higher Self chooses your parents, physical attributes, astrological blueprint and corresponding personality quirks, the world it desires to play in, and the challenges it will seek to triumph over. You, the character, are an instrument through which these lessons are learned. Your Higher Self channels its essence into and through you so it can experience life from your unique lens as if living in a virtual reality.

Comprising your greater essence, your Higher Self is always with and within you, guiding you, supporting you, and sending you more love than you can possibly sense or imagine. How beautiful it is that you are experiencing life from a perspective that is so carefully crafted for you to be able to evolve in the way your soul most yearns to! How fun and exciting it is to take on different roles in this earthside play and watch to see how it all unfolds as it is experienced firsthand.

While you may love and care for your characters when playing a video game and you have fun deciding how to navigate life in their realm, you do not fully identify yourself *as* them. You know and realize that you are so much more than this single avenue of soul expression. You are so much more than your human self that is reading this book.

It's not that you are your "lower self"; it's just that your present consciousness is limited to the plane of existence you are currently on. You are simultaneously existing on other dimensions and levels of consciousness beyond this.

While it is highly beneficial that we do not remember every character and every world we have "played" because it would confuse us and add too much complexity to our experience of life, it is still helpful to connect with the higher consciousness that resides within ourselves when possible. We often become so deeply ingrained in the dramas of our daily lives that we're no longer paying attention to the bigger picture behind it. We may begin to miss out on the whole purpose of the brilliant opportunity we have to be here in this body, as this person, learning the specific lessons that we are. And oh, what a shame *that* is!

Connecting with your Higher Self offers the opportunity to zoom out from the day-to-day worries, fears, pain, pettiness, and suffering and see things from the perspective of the wise, ancient, and unconditionally loving version of ourselves we truly are deep down. This connection can also remind us how much more magical and synchronistic life is than we may have been led to believe and how much more powerful and interesting *we* really are.

Connecting with this deeper layer of consciousness can, unfortunately, be quite difficult in the busy society we live in. Even with a dedicated practice of slowing down, tuning in, and quieting the noise both outside and within our minds, it's incredibly easy to get sucked back into the tangible reality we have gotten so used to and the daily dramas that come along with it. This is why it is helpful to have a tool that can help us briefly step out from the game-like experience that is our lives, bypass our thinking minds, and enter a state of awareness where it is much easier to hear the deep inner voice that lies silently within.

Connecting to the Higher Self with Hypnosis

One of the ways we can bypass our thinking minds and create an opening in our consciousness to receive messages from our Higher Selves is through the use of hypnosis. Although it may sound like it belongs in science fiction, working in trance is a beautiful and sacred process that is not unlike the journey work shamans have already been doing for centuries, where they enter an altered state of consciousness to connect with spirit realms. However, hypnosis does not require any psychedelic drugs, plant medicine, or psychic ability from the practitioner or the client. It works for virtually every person as long as they are willing and open to having the experience.

This is not the type of hypnosis that has become well-known, thanks to popular entertainment, where the hypnotist MC makes suggestions for its participants to bawk like a chicken or do other embarrassing things. The primary purpose, in this case, is for healing and self-discovery. A gentle level of hypnosis allows the client to speak freely and openly about their experiences while tapping into an altered state of consciousness.

Each hypnosis session begins with the client lying down in a comfortable position. They rest on a bed or couch as if getting ready to take a nap. Then, the hypnosis practitioner speaks in a soft, melodic tone using a script that sounds like a guided meditation (or what I like to think of as a magical spell) to induce the client into a trance state. The client becomes so calm and relaxed that, after a while, they gradually begin dreaming while awake.

While in this dream state, healing visions begin to come forth. The questions that have been on the client's mind about the deeper reasons for the issues in their life can finally be answered. They can even discover the answers to more general questions about the nature of spirituality and the inner workings of the universe. The hypnosis practitioner acts as a sacred guide for the client as they journey through this vision quest, ensuring that all the questions brought to the session are answered and the client feels comfortable and held the entire time.

This is a safe and relatively easy process, but what comes through is always incredibly life-altering and often unexpected. Even though the client is asked to come to the session with a list of questions they wish to have answered, the Higher Self always brings forth the most relevant information, according to *its* higher perspective, as the main priority. There is often a stark difference between what the client thinks is most important and what their Higher Self thinks is most relevant, so staying open-minded is key. This is what happens when we are dealing with a consciousness that holds much greater wisdom than we are capable of accessing as our human selves - and one that can see the bigger picture of not only this lifetime but all of them combined!

Often, our Higher Self and team of guides have wanted to bring through many messages for a very long time, so hypnosis sessions are often quite drawn out and in-depth experiences. It is not always easy for the spirit realm to get through to us in our normal waking lives because we are often too distracted and busy, so the guides always tend to have a lot to say.

We don't always remember our dreams (or perhaps we choose not to take a moment to tune into them) when we wake up in the morning. We may not meditate regularly or take enough time in silence to slow down and pay attention to our inner world. The Higher Self is very grateful for every opportunity given to convey a message to their human counterpart, especially when that message can be delivered as clearly as it can be with hypnosis.

When you think of this concept of receiving a message from your Higher Self, you might hope or expect that it will be spoken out loud in a direct and discernible manner that you can easily follow through and take action on. However, the messages that come through via hypnosis take on various creative forms that may not seem very straightforward in the beginning. Because we channel a higher consciousness when under hypnosis, there are not always appropriate words in our human language to convey all that our Higher Selves want to say. Showing us visions and dream-like experiences can be a more effective way for the Higher Self to transmit the higher vibrational messages they have for us. There is also the issue of not always being able to know what we should be asking about since we can only see our situation from our limited human perspective within the "video game."

At the beginning of each hypnosis session, the messages from the Higher Self arrive as visions, sensations, feelings, and emotions. For example, showing a past life can be a common way for the Higher Self to explain some of the issues or ailments the client is currently being affected by in this life. Past lives are one way your Higher Self communicates with you because these experiences overlap with and explain the source of what you are going through right now. We learn more from experience than we do by simply being told information.

It is important to note that your Higher Self and spirit team unconditionally love and respect you and will always do their best to protect you. Everything that comes through is conveyed through the lens and at the level of understanding of the client, as well as what the practitioner can handle. If the concept of past lives is not something the client is accustomed to or feels ready to explore, they simply won't be shown any. They may instead see a past memory from their current lifetime or a fictional dream vision that holds symbolic significance for what they are going through.

The more time a person spends under hypnosis, the more deeply they will enter the trance. While they may start off in a light trance state, they will eventually drop into a deeper trance state as they get used to being under hypnosis. By the end, it is normal for a client to begin channeling direct messages and clear, straightforward answers to the questions being asked of their Higher Self. Even while this is happening, the person may still see images in their mind's eye to help support the clarity of those messages.

The main goal of connecting with the Higher Self is to bring healing and raise our consciousness. It is not to prove whether or not past lives truly exist. Although many people have reported finding proof of events that they witnessed in their past life visions, it doesn't matter if what is seen "really happened" or not. What is important is the moral of the story and the healing that can be gleaned from it in the present lifetime.

INTRODUCTION

How Quantum Hypnosis Works

There are a number of stages within the process of hypnosis. As a client is induced into the dreamlike state that is considered to be a form of hypnotic trance, they will move from the "beta" brainwave state that we are all used to operating from, into the light "alpha" trance state, and eventually the deeper "theta" trance state.

Here's a brief explanation of these common brainwave states that we regularly experience every day:

- BETA - Fully alert and awake. Ego and societal programming rule here. Life feels very tangible and dense, and we are fully immersed in a vivid awareness of our daily lives.

- ALPHA - A light level of trance. We easily and effortlessly move into alpha from the moment we close our eyes and within less than a minute into watching TV. If you have ever seen someone daydreaming while looking out a window or staring into space like they are off with the fairies, you have witnessed alpha in action.

- THETA - The deepest level of trance. It is the state we're in when we're dreaming while we're asleep, and it is the sweet spot where we have access to our subconscious soul memories and this beautiful connection with our Higher Selves. This is also the brainwave state that psychics and mediums can naturally tap into to channel spirits and find answers from the great beyond. The only difference is that, in hypnosis, you can be guided here to find your own answers instead.

- DELTA - Fully asleep, possibly snoring, with the mouth open. There are no dreams being experienced as the body takes a complete rest.

Once someone is under hypnosis and has moved gradually, easily, and effortlessly into the theta brainwave state (trance) and has not gone so far that they have reached the delta (sleeping) state, the Higher Self begins offering visions or other dreamlike experiences that hold deep wisdom for the client. These can be fully immersive experiences where they are aware of all the sensations they would have in their waking life, including the emotions, feelings, and sensations they had in previous lives. It is not uncommon for a person to cry about an experience they had as another "video game character" in another life, even if the situation they see themselves in happened hundreds of years ago.

Being under hypnosis is a drowsy, restful feeling. It's a bit like having a sleepy conversation with a friend while relaxing with your eyes closed. For some, hypnosis can seem quite subtle, and it can be easy to question if they are even under hypnosis because it feels so natural. Others report feeling like there is an "energetic veil" over their eyes that helps them tune out the world around them and direct their attention inward.

During the hypnosis process, the client is deeply relaxed and highly suggestible, but they are not so entrenched in a trance that they cannot get up and use the bathroom or ask for a blanket for warmth if needed. It is not like being under general anesthesia when undergoing surgery. Very rarely does someone not remember anything that happened, as most people are relatively consciously aware throughout the session. Some can even participate in asking questions of their Higher Self along with the practitioner. The session is always recorded because there is so much information that comes through over the course of a few hours that it could be easily forgotten otherwise.

It's important to note that a hypnosis practitioner can only guide someone as deep into a trance as the person will allow themselves to go. It cannot be done without someone's permission or against their will. The client must choose to fully surrender to the experience and trust that it will always bring forth what is in their highest good. Gaining familiarity with guided meditations or right-brain activities such as making art can help someone develop a greater ability to surrender to whatever wishes to come through without questioning it with their logical mind, which may take them out of the experience.

While there is a scientific explanation for how hypnosis works (as illustrated by the different brainwave states mentioned previously), there are also strong mystical components to this New Age modality. There is plenty that cannot always be explained, as hypnotists learn more and more with each session. Our consciousness as humans is ever-evolving! As our ability to understand spirituality expands, the information that comes through continues to meet us at our level of understanding while also pushing us slightly beyond what we could comprehend previously.

These mystical components include the ability to recall past lives, channel messages from ancestors and loved ones who wish to contribute to the session, and even remember lives on other planets and places there is no known record of here on Earth. Additionally, some clients report having extrasensory healing abilities in other lifetimes they may or may not already be aware of in this one.

Yet another mystical component is the energy healing portion that can occur during a hypnosis session. As the session wraps up and all questions have been answered, the Higher Self is invited to bring energetic healing to the client. This healing can take on many forms, whether it is simply a process of energizing the client's body so they feel more vibrant and grounded after the session or speeding up the rate of healing for particular ailments the client has been dealing with for a long time. This part of each session is especially fascinating because the Higher Self can see issues and ailments in the body that even the client themselves were not aware of and share suggestions and energy work to support their healing process. We truly never know what will come up in a session, but we can always trust that it's exactly what is most needed and appropriate for each person.

The Higher Self Explains Itself

Because it is possible to ask the Higher Self questions about absolutely anything you wish in a hypnosis session, I have taken the opportunity as a practitioner to ask about the nature of the Higher Self. It was my hope to better understand who exactly we are working with in hypnosis. Each person I asked to describe the Higher Self did so using their lens of understanding and choice of words while ultimately presenting a similar concept.

Here is what came through with a client, who will be referred to as "C," when in the deepest stages of her hypnosis session:

N: What can you tell us about the nature of the Higher Self?

C: The nature of the Higher Self is that it is the accumulated knowledge and wisdom that has been collected not only across human lifetimes, but other lifetimes in other places. It is also connected to the source, to the creation of the universe. Nothing is separated. That is just a human idea. The Higher Self is universal wisdom that appears to have a human voice, but in reality it is data, stories, perspectives, the birth of the universe. It is intelligence that is higher than human intelligence.

It is a cloud of energy to which wisdom is being drawn from. The information comes through a filter that is understood for the relevant place the human being is at in their life and soul path.

I also took the opportunity to ask this same question in another hypnosis session with "L":

N: What can you tell us about the nature of the Higher Self?

L: It is an aspect that is connected to her in this life, it is connected to her

INTRODUCTION

in all her other lives, and it forms part of the web of all consciousness that is connected back to God, the Goddess, whatever your choice of term is.

Whilst we all understand from a theoretical perspective the web and the nature of humanity, the Higher Self is the one that connects into the super web of consciousness and feeds information down to the consciousness of the human living the reality.

The Higher Self sees all and knows all and filters it down because being able to see all and know all can be too much for humans living in the reality. So, the Higher Self also acts as the filter for always the best and highest good or nature for the human in their lifetime. We are always here.

Others have said the Higher Self's role is to help us learn and push us. This is the energy we are directly speaking with in the hypnosis sessions you will find in this book.

About the Case Studies

Every single session is extraordinary in its own way. Every single session with every client holds special wisdom that is incredibly healing, groundbreaking, profound, and enlightening. The sessions featured in this book were chosen because they can teach us a lot about the nature of the Higher Self and how to become more trusting in this aspect of ourselves. Every person featured also happens to be a healer. I find that these are the type of people who are the most interested in accessing their Higher Self because it is a road towards wholeness.

While you may not always know the context behind each question the client wanted to ask their Higher Self, I hope the Higher Self's answers to each of their questions will widen your understanding of what is possible when it comes to the inner workings of the spirit world and the relationship between you and your own Higher Self. Perhaps some answers will spark more questions than can be answered in this book.

I invite you to stay open-minded and let your subconscious receive the wisdom within these passages, even if not everything is understood on the level of the logical mind.

Please note: These hypnosis sessions are written the way they were originally said based on how each client spoke and how they described what they saw using their own words, so they may not be transcribed in perfect, grammatically correct English.

Sometimes, the hypnotized client will switch pronouns from one sentence to the next, first referring to themselves as "I," then "she/he/they," "we," or even "you." This happens because the client is essentially translating the messages they are receiving in their mind's eye. They also answer questions based on the pronouns used by the practitioner. I have updated some of these pronouns to make who is being referenced more obvious where possible.

As these sessions are always highly personal, each client's name has been shortened to the first letter. My questions and promptings are displayed under "N" for my name, Natalie. Proprietary and personal information, such as copyrighted hypnosis induction scripts, people, places, or locations, have been removed. Otherwise, everything is transcribed verbatim exactly as it occurred in the session so you can immerse yourself in the full experience of the healing visions and messages that have come forth from the Higher Self.

Chapter 2:
My First Session

When my first hypnosis session occurred, I was going through a big transition in my work. I was beginning to focus on doing less and not working as hard, which was something I had been putting a lot of thought towards for some time. It was as if my soul was tired and knew there had to be a better way than to slave away at a computer helping others all day, something I had been doing for many years. I was ready to simplify, downsize, and allow room in my schedule to follow my intuition and invite in more ease and flow.

I didn't even think to mention this situation in the questions I gave Valerie, my hypnosis practitioner, to ask my Higher Self while I was under hypnosis. However, this need to reimagine my approach to work ended up becoming one of the main aspects my Higher Self wanted to focus on. It turned out that the issue of becoming too obsessed with work had been a key subject across multiple lifetimes, and I was about to discover it was something I needed to become more aware of in the 6-hour session that would follow.

Having recently discovered hypnosis as a modality for connecting with the Higher Self, my main intention for this first session was simply to have an experience. I wanted to learn more about myself and the universe. I also brought a handful of random questions about many different aspects of my life. These were asked in rapid-fire succession at the end of the session. While all my questions did get answered, what I ended up learning from my Higher Self was even more extraordinary.

I learned that the past lives we experience tend to follow a pattern - like a pendulum swinging from one side to another. At first, we may go too far in one direction with our approach to a certain area of our lives. Then, the pendulum swings in the other direction, and we may choose to express the complete opposite behavior in the next life as we gradually seek balance. This is a theme that comes up over and over in hypnosis sessions. It's pretty amazing that the Higher Self has the ability to see these patterns from a bird's eye view and set up situations in our current lives to help bring harmony to areas that are out of balance.

On the day of my first hypnosis session, I was nervous and excited. Valerie deBeaumont, my practitioner, met me outside with a huge smile and welcomed me into her office, where we began talking and getting to know each other for a couple of hours. I shared my intentions for the session, and she answered any questions I had. We were having such a good time talking that I felt very safe in her presence and knew I would be in good hands.

As the hypnosis portion begins, I am lying down on a couch, covered in a soft, white, fluffy blanket, with a couple of pillows under my head. I feel comfortable and peaceful as Valerie sits on a chair beside me. She has a stack of notes on her lap, including her induction script and the questions I brought to my session. Those questions will not be asked until after my Higher Self has an opportunity to display a series of visions to convey the bigger message it wishes to impart, something neither the practitioner nor I will be able to predict.

The induction begins with Valerie offering a few easy visualization practices and relaxation-deepening techniques. She invites me to imagine I am floating on a cloud. Eventually, she guides me back down to the surface, where I subtly glide into my first vision.

MY FIRST SESSION

V: I want you to tell me the very first thing you see below you or the very first impression that you get as you come back down to the surface.

N: Snow. Snow blowing. It's like there's so much snow, and it will never end.

V: How does your body feel in this place as you settle into the scene? Taking your time, would you say that your body feels male or...?

N: Male. Middle-aged. Strong.

V: Okay. And as you settle into that body and feel into it, look down at your feet. Looking at your hands, what do you notice that you're wearing?

N: Like, fur boots?
   My hands are... I look like I work hard. I'm strong, but there's way too much work to do and it will never end.
   There are big mountains off in the distance. There is snow on them, and they're really beautiful.

V: Do you get the sense that you're carrying anything with you or on you?

N: I'm wearing a jacket, kind of puffy, and I'm using something to move the snow.

V: Okay, and that jacket - how does it feel to you? Can you tell what it's made out of?

N: Navy blue. It's kind of like a feather down. It doesn't seem that thick, but I don't feel cold.

V: Okay. What do you get the sense that you're doing in this place?

N: Working. And it feels pointless. It just feels like it's just gonna snow again. I can do it and I'll just keep doing it, but I'm doing it by myself. Like nobody's helping me.

V: And how does that make you feel?

N: It feels like it's my job.

I can sense a family far in the distance inside. I don't know what they're doing. But I feel like this is my responsibility, and it's never gonna get done.

V: Yes. Do you have certain tools or devices that you're using?

N: A shovel.

I feel like I'm gonna be doing this for the rest of my life. It's endless.

V: Let's see where it is that this man resides, where he spends a good deal of his time when he's not working. We're going to move forward, to see where this man resides, where he spends much of his time, moving to where this man resides. Be there now.

N: I'm holding a baby, like a toddler. I'm a dad. It's a very small house.

V: Tell me about the house.

N: There's a woman sweeping.

I feel like I don't get to be home that much. I don't know my kids that well because I don't get to spend that much time with them.

V: How does he feel when he is there? How does this moment feel for him?

N: He's sort of nonchalant. Like it's not gonna last. I'm going to have to go back to work.

V: Yes. How many children does it appear that he has?

N: There's a little toddler, and a young boy, and another girl. There might be more, I don't know.
   I heard five. (Laughs)

V: Tell me a little bit about this house.

N: It's brown, like a wood brown. I'm sitting at a dining room table on a wooden chair, bouncing a toddler [on my knee]. There's a kitchen to my right. I can see a bed in the next room.

V: Would you say that this is a modern house? How would you describe this home?

N: Quaint? It feels like it's far away in nature.

V: Is it like a wood cabin?

N: Yeah. There's a wood stove.
   There's dogs! Sleigh dogs. I like my dog. I think the sleigh is red. I feel like I'm closer with the dog than my family because we spend a lot of time working.
   Chopping wood... [there's] just so much work. That's like my big takeaway from all of this. (Laughs) And it's only me doing it, and it's my duty, and I don't get to be a part of the family as much.

V: It's having to be a provider.

N: Yeah. But it feels pointless. I'm just kinda going through the motions.

V: Let's close the door on this scene. We're going to move forward to another day in this man's life that is important for you to see today. Moving forward to another day that is important for you to see. Be there now.

N: My daughter's older. She's getting married, and I'm realizing that my hard work... (Trails off and bursts into tears)

V: You're fine. It's all right to let it flow. It's okay to feel this.

N: (Continues crying deeply for a few minutes) I spent years feeling like it didn't matter, but it really mattered. (Breathing deeply through tears)
 Because I was out there doing all the work, they got to live their lives. And accomplish things and feel nurtured.
 It's almost like I'm finally now realizing it. And for many years, I just felt super... like... "Screw this." And I'm just seeing how beautiful she is and happy and how protected she's felt.

V: What a beautiful moment.

N: I think I'm probably crying at her wedding or something. It feels overwhelming. And now she's gonna make a really good wife to a man who's gonna do great things.

V: Yes. He's lucky to have felt that.

N: Yeah. He feels like he was in his head and he disconnected himself from his family. It wasn't actually how things were. His wife wanted to be closer to him... or me. But I just felt like, eh, I'm just a worker.

V: He's lucky to have that revelation.

N: Yeah.

V: We're gonna close the door on this beautiful scene and we're going to move forward to another day in this man's life that is important for you to see today. Moving forward, be there now.

N: I'm old, and there's a little boy handing me a toy. Maybe a grandchild. I'm smiling, and I'm... I'm softened. And I'm enjoying being with him. I care more. I don't feel pressure to do anything. I'm just present.

V: Does he feel good about his life?

N: (Deep sigh) He's happy about where he is now. Peaceful.
    I don't know if he has a health problem. I feel shaky in this area... my heart.

V: Do you get the sense that he's coming to the end of his life?

N: Yeah. I think he knows something's wrong with it. Maybe that's why he's enjoying the moment.

V: Yes. We're gonna go ahead and move forward to the last day in this man's life. Looking forward to the last day. Be there now.

N: I'm laying in bed with a red blanket. It feels like... [my death happened] just quick... I'm not expecting [it]. And I just go. But I was expecting it... just not at that moment. It seems like a single bed.

V: Were there others he was living with at the time?

N: I don't know. It feels like the house is quiet.

V: Does he feel ready to go?

N: I get the sense he doesn't care about much... in life... most of it. He was just doing what he had to do. So, it didn't really bother him. He's not holding onto a lot. I feel like he did what he was there to do.

V: Is he ready to let go of this life?

N: Yeah, he's floating.

V: Okay. Taking a deep breath in, we're going to release from this lifetime, release from that body, floating away from that body with immense gratitude for all that life has shown and we're drifting away.

And as we drift away from that lifetime, we can see it from a different point of view. As we look back at that life and see it from a different perspective, what do you think you learned from that life?

N: Just to focus on work. But it was a very peaceful setting, a very peaceful place. No one was yelling at me to do the work. It was just my duty. I feel like I learned about doing a duty on behalf of others. And that it did matter, but I didn't really get to have a life. It was for them... for them to experience life.

V: Yes. Beautiful.

N: But my heart kind of just tinged. Like I didn't let enough love out.

V: So there's a lesson in that life.

MY FIRST SESSION

As this exchange was happening, I felt very amused that I knew the answers to every question Valerie asked me. The answer always dropped in the moment she finished asking, as if by magic. I was surprised to hear my quick and easy replies as the voice from within me described these situations so vividly.

I felt very connected to this first vision I was shown because it explains why I have felt such a strong compulsion to spend my days helping others in my current lifetime. Performing a duty on behalf of others has become a source of comfort for me and a beautiful way I choose to express myself. However, now I do that work with a feeling of love in my heart and am able to focus on the creatively fulfilling projects I am most passionate about for my own benefit as well as others, which is a step up from that previous lifetime.

That shift did not happen immediately upon entering my current lifetime. I was about to see another past life where I started learning to enjoy being of service to others more, but I went so overboard with it that I failed to allow them to be of service to me in return. I did not nourish myself as well as I could have as a result.

N: I first saw myself young and dancing, but now I'm knitting and I'm older. And I'm just doing it for fun. I feel like there's a lot of people in my life that I love.

V: As you feel into that body, tell me more.

N: I'm knitting to keep my family warm, and I'm putting love into my work. And I don't even need to make it. I'm just doing it because it's fun.

V: And in this scene, as you feel into this body as a female, how old does that body feel?

N: I have curly gray hair, and I feel like I loved my family really well this time. I'm a very nurturing person, and I'm somebody they can talk to.

V: And does this body feel strong, or does it feel weak? I know it feels older, but how does that older body feel?

N: She... she feels like she can still do everything.

V: Okay. And tell me a little bit about her surroundings. What do you notice about where she finds herself?

N: It seems similar to the last house... wooden, but there's a garden outside. Glass doors that go to the garden.

V: And who does she share this house with?

N: Um, I think she lives alone here now, but I get the sense that she has at least one daughter. She's very involved in her life. Maybe too much. (Giggles)
    It's kind of like the other way around [compared to the last life where I barely knew my children].

V: The other direction, yes.

N: Yeah, but she's happy about it. But everything she does is thinking about them... or *her*? Maybe the daughter's the one she's the closest with.

V: Is her daughter there with her?

N: No, I get the feeling like I'm gonna prepare something for her.

V: Okay, beautiful. Let's close the door on this scene and we're going to move forward to another day in this woman's life that is important for you to see today. Moving forward to another day, be there now.

N: I'm sick, and people are serving me... on fancy plates... like a tea party. And I can't get up to help. People are serving me, and I don't like it. I'm having to receive now, and it feels very uncomfortable.

V: Ah, interesting.

N: I'm like, "I want to go get things, make things, bake things." But they're like, "Sit down."

V: Okay. So, she's used to doing and not receiving. Who is it that she's with in this scene?

N: There's a whole table of people... women, my daughter, family and friends. People from the church? (Surprised by this answer)
And I feel like I might not get better, so I'm flustered because I want to help. My body's breaking down, and I'm having to get used to not doing so much.

V: Okay. So, she's having to give up some duties.

N: Yeah. And she won't speak up about what she needs because she doesn't want people to do things for her.

V: Why doesn't she want to ask for help?

N: She wants to do things herself.

V: Those people around her are willing to help her, aren't they?

N: Oh yeah. They want her to let them help her! (Laughs)

V: She's just very independent, isn't she?

N: I think she finally found joy in helping. She doesn't wanna let it go, because it's the only way she knows how to get joy. Or it's what she's used to.

V: Was there a time in her life where she wasn't joyful about helping?

N: When she was young, she had to help her siblings. And she resented it at first, but then she learned to enjoy it more... taking care of little ones... and it helped her be a good mom later.

When we first started, I saw myself dancing at my wedding, and I was very happy. I had a big, flowing dress and long, blonde hair. And it one of the best days of my life because then I could become a mom and have my own children. I feel like the focus is mostly on nurturing my daughter, but there might be more.

V: Let's go back in time to find out a little bit more about this woman's life and her younger days when she was married with young children. Moving back in time to find out more about her life with being married with children, be there now.

N: (Goes back into childhood instead) I'm like a tomboy... I like to learn how to do things on the farm, and it was fun to learn. If I got a new task, it felt like an honor because it's like I graduated.

But then, all of a sudden, I had too much responsibility. Something with my parents... that's why I had to take care of my siblings.

V: What happened with her parents?

N: I don't know... maybe my dad is still there, but my mom is gone. But my dad is very angry and sad.

V: Let's go a little bit deeper into this scene. I'm gonna count from three to one, and with each number, you're going to be deeper and more clear in this scene. 3... going deeper... 2... even deeper still... 1... deeper and more clear than it has ever been before.

N: My mom is gone. My name is Dorothy, and I don't do things as good as my mom did them. Now that she's gone—she died in childbirth with another sibling—my dad's kind of annoyed because I'm not as good at helping as my mom was.

V: How old do you feel?

N: Teenager. And I had been a tomboy, but now I needed to learn how to be in the house. I wanted to help with the farm, but now I have to take care of my siblings and learn how to cook, and I'm not good at it. (Laughs)

V: Ah, okay. So, you were kind of forced into a role that you didn't want.

N: I think I wanted it. I just wasn't used to it. And that's probably why I went overboard with it later [on in life], because I wanted to prove that I'm super nurturing.

I'm sad about my mom leaving, too, because now no one's there to nurture me. And my dad's not nice—but I know he's just hurting—and that makes me miss my mom. (Crying) Why did she have to have another baby?

V: Did the baby survive?

N: I don't think so. I am grateful because then I might have to take care of it.

V: Oh, okay. Right. Are there other siblings?

N: Yeah, at least two.

V: Are you the oldest?

N: Yeah. I'm quite a bit older. I think I'm a young teenager. I had to grow up really fast.

V: And in those years of being a young teenage girl, what do you notice about your surroundings? What do you wear? What timeframe does it seem like to you?

N: 1800s. There's a farm and horses, and dresses that have lacey little parts on the front. And a bonnet. We'd wear a bonnet when we went out.

V: Yes. And your siblings, are they boys or girls?

N: I just remember a lot of runny noses, and it's gross. (Both laugh) And I have to always fix their noses. I think a little boy.

V: Is there anyone in this family that you feel closer to than others?

N: I'm with the kids a lot, but they're not on my level. I feel like I'm missing that nurturing, but I had it growing up.

V: And as you look at your dad, are you close with him at all?

N: I used to like being around him, but I don't anymore. Because he ridicules me for not doing things as good.

V: Can you see your father's face? (Yeah.)
   I know they often say that the eyes are the windows to the soul. And if you look into his eyes, is he anybody that you recognize?

N: (Bursts out crying) My mom [in my current lifetime].

V: Okay, tell me how that makes you feel.

N: She's mean in this life, too!

V: Okay, well, we know she didn't mean to be.

N: Yeah. She goes through a hard time and she doesn't deal with it well.

V: Yes, yes, yes.

N: (Still crying) I wanted to help on the farm, but now I can't do it anymore.

V: How does that make you feel?

N: Well, I'm learning to reroute my desires into a different area. It was hard at first, but as I get older, I'm learning to love helping with the home.

V: Yes. Just had to change gears.

N: I get better at it over time and I learn how to make the recipes right.
   And there's a softening… the longer the time passes from my mom's

passing [from that lifetime].

V: And do things improve with the father?

N: He's still distant. But he doesn't really ridicule me as much. I'm doing really good now, and I'm pleasing him more.

V: Yes. I'm gonna close the door on this scene. I'm going to move forward to another day in this young woman's life that is important for you to see today. Moving forward to another day, be there now.

N: A boy handed me a flower.
    I started to realize there's a life outside of the home I grew up with, and I can create my own home. I'm so relieved that my siblings are getting older, and I won't always have to be in that role. And I can create my own home because... (crying) he wants to marry me.

V: Do you decide to marry?

N: Yeah. There's not even like a thought.

V: Let's find out a little bit more about what this life was like together with him. Tell me more about that relationship.

N: I don't know... I don't feel like he's a big part. I'm so focused on my children, but I don't feel pain or sadness about him. I don't know.

V: Let's go a little bit deeper into that relationship with that husband in that lifetime and get a better idea of how that was. I'm gonna count backwards from three to one, and with each number, you're gonna be even more clear on this. 3... going deeper... 2... even deeper still... 1... deeper and clearer than you have ever been before.

N: I feel like… only a couple years into our marriage, he found another woman, but I don't feel upset because I got the life I wanted. And to me, that's who he was. A ticket to my new life.

I don't know if I'm hiding from something or not, though. I think I just really wanted to be a mom, to have my own children, and raise them with love. And that's what I'm getting to do, so I'm not sad. And I don't think we got to spend a lot of time together, so I don't think it feels like a big loss.

V: And how many children did you have?

N: The daughter is very strong to me, but I feel like I took care of other kids, too. I don't know if they're mine…it feels like they're cousins. Maybe there is a boy, too.

V: But the daughter is the one that stands out the most. (Yeah.)
Tell me about her.

N: I just see long hair.
She always has some kind of problem, and I rush to help. And I love it. It might be my stepsister in this life.

V: Take some time to look into her eyes and feel her soul. What does she feel like to you?

N: She feels like my stepsister [in the current lifetime].
(Referring back to past life) I always like to hear what's on her mind. I help her with boys and getting ready for school and everything. And it's like my main focus.

And nothing she says is silly. I don't ever think, "I'm sick of helping you." I always feel like, "What more..? What can I...? What else can I do? Do you need this?" And I spend my whole day prepping things so that she can have a good life. And I'm happy about it.

V: Lucky girl.

N: But I'm sure she probably feels smothered sometimes. Like, can you have your own life? (Laughs)
So, that's why I was knitting. Because I'm like, here's my hobby... but I'm making something for you!

Interesting to note: In my current life, my stepsister is someone I usually have a very strong compulsion not to help. This is probably a way to make up for this previous imbalance where I went overboard with helping her.

V: Let's close the door on this scene. We're going to move forward to another day in this woman's life that's important for you to see today. Moving forward to another day, be there now.

N: I'm at the very end, and I need people to help me. I actually have to ask.

V: How does that make her feel?

N: Like I wanna roll my eyes. But I can't not ask. So, it's kind of painful. It's pushing me out of my comfort zone. If I need water, I have to ask. And my mouth is so dry because I don't want to ask.

V: Are there other people around her, though, happy to help?

N: Yeah. They're looking at me concerned. "What can I do for her?"

V: Is she lying down? Is she sitting up?

N: Lying down. She's very weak. She can barely even sit up. She has to be spoon fed. And they're like, "Do you want more?" And she doesn't wanna say if she wants more or not. She does. But she doesn't want to say that she does. So, she started robotically asking, "Water." "More." She's resigned herself to the fact that she just has to.

V: Who are the ones that are caring for her in this time?

N: A nurse. It's like a hospice-type setting.
  Even though they're not my kids, I still don't want them to help me. But my daughter visits me. I can't respond to her very well.

V: When you feel into that body, what feels wrong with that body?

N: Well, I'm just really old and weak. My bones are very stiff.

V: Is she sensing that the end is near?

N: Yeah, but she's just so upset that people are helping her. She doesn't even think about that. Most of her mind is on like, "Oh no, they're gonna come in and do this for me."

V: I see. Let's go ahead and move forward to the last day in this woman's life. Moving forward to the last day. Be there now.

N: I feel like I'm sleeping and that's when I go. But maybe I'm just always sleeping because I don't feel good. They tried to feed me, but I said no. I'm done with this place. (Laughs)

V: Is she feeling ready to let go of this lifetime? (Yeah.)
  Okay. You're gonna take a deep breath in, and when you exhale, release from that lifetime, release from that body, releasing from that

lifetime and letting it float away. And as we drift away from that lifetime, we give this woman much thanks and much gratitude for showing us her experience and for sharing her emotions with us. We're very grateful.

And as we have the opportunity to see this lifetime from a different perspective, what are some of the lessons learned from that life?

N: I learned how to be a loving woman. I'm very grateful. I didn't nourish myself as much as I could have. I gave of myself too much. But I loved it. (Smiles)

V: Yes. Beautiful, beautiful lessons.

N: But I went too far.

V: Well, that's alright. She did a good job.

N: Yes, especially if you think about the [life] before that.

V: Yes, yes. We're so grateful for that.

We're going to go ahead and move away from that lifetime. Moving away. We're going to drift and float and float and drift so much gratitude for all that we're seeing today. And as we drift, we're looking for the next appropriate time and place that is important for you to see today.

I had now seen a second lifetime where I tried to correct my behavior from the first lifetime I was shown. As someone who had previously felt their work did not matter and experienced an emotional disconnect from the people he was doing a duty on behalf of in the first lifetime shown, I then chose to have a lifetime where I could be of service to my family in a very open-hearted, loving way as a woman. However, I went a bit overboard with that lesson, too. I now needed to work on learning how to allow others to serve and assist me when I need help.

Now, Valerie moves me forward into the next segment of the session. Here, I experience yet another past life that merges the qualities of the first two in an attempt to find balance between them both, as a softer, more loving man who was once again very obsessed with his work for the purpose of providing for his family. This story has an interesting twist, however, because this man was my great-great-grandfather.

Born in the late 1800s, my great-great-grandfather immigrated from Norway to the United States. There, he met his wife, married, and had four little girls. Sadly, he passed away early, leaving his wife to raise their children on her own. This was a planned lesson for him just as much as it was for her, as he stayed behind to help as a spirit long after he died.

N: I see a flapper in the twenties. I love music. I really love music, and it feels like life's a party.

V: Tell me about how old you feel.

N: I don't feel like I have kids. I feel independent. Young adult.

V: Okay, so her body feels vibrant? Tell me more.

N: I feel like I might... I don't know if I'm... am I him or am I her?

V: Well, we have all of these beautiful guides gathered here today for this session. So, we're gonna ask for some higher assistance and some clarity. Bringing in that clarity of understanding why we're seeing what we're seeing, why you're having the experience.

Valerie takes several minutes to help me go deeper into hypnosis.

N: I'm him. (Feeling emotional) I'm watching her dance.

I smell wood. I'm really admiring a violin... that I make or make something for. And I put so much love into my work.

It's kind of like a merging of the other two lives. Because I'm a man, but I'm more soft. And I love my children, but my family relies on me and there's so many.

V: Really? How many? Are there lots of children?

N: Lots of little girls.

V: Tell me about the making of the violin and the passion he feels for that.

N: The craftsmanship and the little details and all the little sounds they make, I just feel very attuned to. I can tell when the slightest thing is off, and I'm kind of OCD about it. But that's why people come to me. Because I'm so good at it.

V: Does he love the music of a violin, as well as the craftsmanship?

N: All music, but he's very skilled with the violin. His father taught him. It makes him feel close to his father.

V: Does he feel there's an importance to the music, or does he see value in music?

N: Yeah. Sometimes he doesn't always get to fully enjoy it because he can notice so much. Some people can just sit and listen. And he's like, "Oh, something's wrong with that or this."

V: Yes. Yes. Tell me more about how he feels and more about his life.

N: It's not always easy to make ends meet, but when he does make money, he makes a lot, so they have to make it last. Because it's a skill to play the violin. Not anybody can pick it up.

I feel like... (thinking) before I thought I was the wife because he watches over her after he passed.

I might be my great-great-grandfather. It relates to a lot of my maternal line, issues that many of us face. Wanting to be very independent, but not being able to because we have responsibility.

V: There's a reason why you're seeing this today. Tell me more about what you're seeing.

N: I get the sense that maybe he had thought [in his pre-life planning process] about being the wife [who loses her husband] because it would help him learn that [life is] not all about doing everything for your kids, but he was scared to take [the loss of a spouse] on firsthand, so he wanted to observe it. He's the one who left the family early.

V: Did he pass away? (Yeah.)

Note: In the previous lifetime as the woman who only ever wanted to be a mother, I did not seem upset by losing my husband to another woman. The loss of a spouse in this lifetime was meant to assist with bringing about a greater appreciation for the relationship with a spouse through the experience of losing them.

V: Okay. I'd like to visit some important days in that man's life. I'm gonna go back in time to his earlier life and we'd like to see an important day in that man's life moving back in time. Be there now.

N: I see someone playing piano and I'm young. It just seems like the coolest thing you could do. And people love it. People have a good time because of it. So, it feels like it's my aspiration to work with music. But at this point, it's piano.

V: Ah, I see. How old does he feel in this scene?

N: Like eight? Seven.

V: So, watching music makes an impact on him?

N: And he sees the impact it makes on others. And how it brings them joy.

V: Is there something about this day that is special to him?

N: I think he just realized how much joy it brings him. The piano. Like, "Ooh, this is what life is all about."

V: Is it just piano? Is it music in general?

N: I don't know if there's more instruments playing.

V: But he's impacted by the piano.

N: Yeah. It's a parlor, and he's like, "I'm allowed to be here [at this party]?!" It feels very exciting.

V: How would you describe the music being played?

N: Classical. I'm wearing a little suit, and people are dressed up and dancing, and they have bright lipstick.

V: Does he wanna dance, too?

N: No, he's sitting and his knee is going up and down. He just thinks it's the coolest thing he's ever seen.

V: Yes. Amazing. We're gonna close the door on this scene. We're going to move forward to another day in that lifetime that is important for you to see. Moving forward to another day. Be there now.

N: He met his wife, and she likes music, too! He loves her. He thinks she's so beautiful. That's kind of how he felt about piano. (Laughs)

V: Okay! He knows something good when he sees it.

N: He wants to make a life with her. There's a lot of talk about his work. His business. It's stressful. He's realizing if he wants to start a family, he's gonna have to step things up.

V: Gotcha, gotcha.

N: Because he's so obsessed with detail, and he has to make a lot of them. He's going to have to not be so attached, and keep up the quality of the work. And he's kind of stressed about that, but he'll do anything for her.

V: Okay. He loves her.
   I'm gonna close the door on this scene. We're going to move forward to another day in that lifetime that is important for you to see today. Moving forward, be there now.

N: The third baby was just born. It's such a miracle, but he can't help but feel some pressure that there's another person to take care of. He's achieved more than he ever thought he could because of the inspiration of his family. And now he's like, "Can I do another level of this?" So, it's mixed emotions. Like, "Yay, beautiful... but oh crap, I've got to really figure this out."

But because of that, he steps it up and he does really, really well [financially]. I see him being very successful now... in a way he didn't think he could be. So, the baby is like a catalyst. He's doing really well. They have more money coming in than they need.

V: Okay, so he has done very well.

N: Yes, and they can have more children if they want. So they do. And he's not worried anymore.

V: Okay, he's done well!

We're gonna close the door on this scene. I'm gonna move forward to another day in this man's life that is important for you to see today. Moving forward to another day, be there now.

N: I feel like he might have died… (Worried)

V: Okay. It's alright.

N: He's not... he's shocked.

V: He's shocked that he died?

N: It was a surprise for everybody.

V: When you feel into that situation, how does it feel that he may have passed? Is it something physical? Or was it an accident?

N: I don't know, but I feel like I... it was planned.

V: Planned on a soul level? (Yeah.)
　Well, let's find out how this man died.

N: He feels sick.

V: Okay. Was it a short sickness or a long sickness... something sudden or something long and drawn out?

N: Sudden. Short. I can't work.
　I'm worried about my work, but not myself... which is silly because that's how you work... is by being able to.
　But I feel like it was planned. And now I get to watch what happens with everybody.

*Note: My great-great-grandfather died from pneumonia in his early 40s.

V: How does he feel when he watches? How does he feel being out of that body? Does he stick around for a while to watch his family?

N: He helps. It's like he's there, but he's not. At first he felt like, "Oh no, I'm used to doing so much, and now I can't help."
　But then he realized over time he *can* help, just not in the same way. He's still helping to line up opportunities and people to help.
　But everybody's *so* not doing well.

V: Because he's left?

N: Yeah. It was their source of income. They can't make any more, so... they're selling off what they have left and they're selling things they didn't want to sell. I see them carrying out paintings. It's just very sad.

V: How does he feel about this from a different perspective?

N: He wants to learn from it, but he's very connected to their emotions. But he knows this was meant to happen.

He talks to them in their dreams, but he can't always get through. He wants them to know he's still there, but they don't know.

V: From this perspective of him trying to talk to them from the spirit side to their physical side, is he able to tell what would help them be able to hear him?

N: Well, I see my great-grandma as a teenager... of course, I did not know her then... and she's playing music.

I feel like he's feeling that she's feeling that they're reconnecting when she plays music. And she plays piano, but she used to play violin, and he guides her to find the right keys. There's lots of sad moments, but he has that joy of music still.

V: Would you say that it's in moments of joy that they can feel him?

N: She probably just thinks it's her intuition or that, because she was raised with music, it comes easily... which is also true. But he does help, and I feel like she has to sense it. She's so good, and she's getting all these opportunities to play for bigger and bigger places.

V: Is this when she's a younger woman or...

N: I see her older.

V: After he's passed?

N: Yeah. I want to say she's probably like 19, but I feel like the age doesn't matter because it's a long story, and he was there for all of it.

It's like he's helping in a different way where he's not so overburdened.

It's not too much. He's still trying to figure out how to help more, but he can only do it subtly now. He doesn't wanna take away from their lessons.

V: Does he feel less pressure?

N: Yeah. He feels like there is a breakthrough, and this is how things were meant to be. But he didn't always feel that way because it's hard to see them struggle. But they learned how to get through it, and they're doing well and living good lives and having their own families. Now he feels like, "Okay, I'm good."

V: Does he feel like he's able to kind of move on?

N: Yeah. He can still pop in if he wants, but it doesn't feel like there's a purpose to. Like he did what he was there to do.

V: Yes. I understand. This is a very special, special life viewing.
   What does he want you to know?

N: (In a pleading voice) It's not about the obsession with the work. It's the effect it has.
   It makes sense because I'm getting ready to move into a new phase in my business right now that's much more hands-off. So, it makes sense that this is the string that would come up right now.
   So yes, there was so much joy from the creation of [music], but that wasn't the point. And the fact that it kind of took away from his own enjoyment at times... he needed to be a little less obsessed with the details.

V: What else does he want you to know? What are some of the lessons or guidance he wants you to know from him showing you this today?

N: Your family still loves you even if they're not always around. (Crying)

And that maybe you are learning more [without them nearby].

Because family has been a big distraction for me [in previous lifetimes]... in a good way, because that was what it was meant to be. But it got pushed aside more in [my current lifetime] because I wanted to focus on my work and helping more people than just my family. Helping as many people as I can. Which would make it really hard if I was very attached to people.

V: Yes. What other wisdom does he want to impart on you?

N: He helped people through the music, but music is a vibration. And [as an astrologer,] I help people just go straight to the vibration.

V: Yes. There's a link there, isn't there?

N: It's more direct.

V: Beautiful, beautiful.

N: In my family that I'm in now, they all love music. So, I didn't lose it. But it's not the focus.

V: Is there anything else that he'd like you to know?

N: Don't focus so much on your tools. It's about the effect. Now my craft is more intellectual, but the computer kind of gets in the way. I'm too obsessed with the computer.

My aura, my words heal. It's not like the little graphics, or the emails, and the clicking, and the messages I am always responding to. Being present for people.

V: Yes. What a beautiful connection.

N: He feels relief that I'm understanding.

V: Okay. Has he been trying to communicate with you before today?

N: I don't know. I'm not aware of that. I often get [spirit] communications from my grandparents, but I never knew him, so I don't know. If he does, I'm not conscious of them.

Oh, I recently picked up my ukulele yesterday, and it was broken. And I emailed the company to say, "Hey, it's broken. Can you fix it?" And they're like, "We'll send you the part, and you can fix it." I just said today to someone, "Why do they think *I* can fix it?" (Laughs)

V: Oh, that's interesting.

N: Apparently, I can!

V: Well, you have some family genetics in there that will help guide you with that. What a beautiful story. I love that. Is there anything else that he would like you to know today before we move on?

N: He says my great-grandma's with me. (Crying)

That was his eldest daughter. She's helping me like he helped her.

V: Yes. Well, let's just feel her love right now. Feel her love and her guidance and her support.

N: She's like, "I didn't die!" (Laughs and sniffles)

V: Well, yes. What else does she want you to know?

N: "Accept help." Because she didn't either. My great-grandma, my grandma, my mom... we don't accept help.

She just says, "I'm with you. I'll be with you, and your [future] son, and continue the music." Even if it's not me [working with music], I can nurture the music in others.

V: Yes. What else does she want you to know?

N: My grandpa came in. He's like, "I'm here, too." And he said, "Good job. Good job." I have a lot of dreams about him, but I don't see my great-grandma [in my dreams] very much. And when I have seen her in my dreams, I tell her to go away.

V: Why do you tell her to go away?

N: I'm like, "You're dead!" Then, I wake up, and I feel really bad.

V: You have a wonderful ancestral support system for you.

N: Yeah, that makes sense, because I got a psychic reading and they said I need to talk to my ancestors. And I didn't understand.

V: Well, they certainly have made themselves known here today. What a beautiful interaction and a beautiful history.

N: It's cool to see the pattern. Like you go a little too far in one direction, and then you push back. You just keep doing that and it's like the vibration on a string. It's just kind of steadying itself.

V: Yes, yes. Beautiful imagery and vibration.

N: My great-grandma's husband, Orvie, came in. (Chuckles)

V: What does he want you to know?

N: He's like, "I'm here, too." He's like, "Don't think of me as being so harsh." Because I was a little girl when he passed and he would swear a lot, and my parents would cover my ears. So, that's how I remember him... as being kind of brash.

V: What does he want you to know about him?

N: He's like, "Don't think of me that way. I'm funny. I'm lighthearted." He knows that he could be too much sometimes, but I would close myself off from connecting with him because [as a little girl] I thought, "My parents say you're not good."

V: So, he's softened that connection for you?

N: Yeah, he said, "It's not so serious." But he's here for me, too, even though we didn't have a good or a big connection.

V: I know that right now we have this beautiful assembly, this beautiful gathering of ancestors here for you today. And I'd love for them... because they have this beautiful access with infinite wisdom... I would love for them to communicate any wisdom that they have for you. Anything that they'd like you to know today?

N: Go back to my art.
    They motioned to a whole room of all of my great-grandma's sisters (all of the little girls that were offspring of the violin maker). And they're all with me and us, and they're all very artistic.
    And they're saying, "Go back to your art. It's not all about work and helping people. You need to nourish yourself with stuff that isn't about making a living." It's not to support people. It's just for fun. And just the joy of creating joy. It seems like it's not important, but it is. It is.

V: What do they want you to know about joy?

N: It's simple. It's not something you achieve. It's something you allow in.

And the colors, they'll heal me, and help me come back to, like, God or Source. I'm seeing a loop drawn. Because I did a meditation where I was asked to go to my origin. I was just a spark of light, and I was making all these beautiful colors. And I did that forever, and [the guides were] like, "Okay, you're getting really smart. You need to move on." So, it was like a loop, like the art brings me back to that essence before I had to learn about the nuances of the universe and responsibilities.

Painting. (Cries)

V: Painting. Okay.

N: And you can just paint over the same painting over and over. It's not about art that you hang in your home. It's the process.

V: I'd love for your ancestors to... again, they have this beautiful connection to infinite wisdom as we all do... would they be willing to answer some questions today or would they like us to contact the Higher Self for some more...

N: (Interrupts) I hear Higher Mind.

V: Higher Mind. Okay. Alright. I'd like to go ahead and connect more deeply with the Higher Self, but before we do, is there anything else that the ancestors would like us to know right now?

N: They just said to build my own easel and put a lot of care into it. It's not about the actual painting. It's like the preparation of the painting, the smell of the wood of the easel. Getting the brushes out. That's all part of the process.

And they said I can talk to my guides while I paint. And it's not about the outcome. They're just really driving that home. They're repeating it...

V: It's the process. Not the outcome.

N: Yeah. Like they're poking me. 'Cause they know how [perfectionistic] I am about that kind of thing.

V: Beautiful. And when you bring more joy into your life, how does that help you?

N: I won't be so attached to the pain here. It's not a problem to solve here. It's an experience to have. Not to get lost in the drama. Smell the air, enjoy the environment. That's how you transcend. I feel very peaceful.

V: Let's take some time in this peacefulness and let me know anything else that they are communicating to you.

N: Slow down, throw out the calendar. You've done enough. They're just like, "You've worked enough! If you stopped working now, it would be okay." (Laughs)

V: Do they know if any of these things have a relationship to some of your physical challenges?

N: That seems to be a different area. Like out of their scope.

V: We will talk to the Higher Self about that. What else would [your ancestors] like you to know today?

N: They said they're having a great time. "Don't worry about us. We're just rooting for you all."

V: When you want some fun help with painting, will they be there for you or with you?

N: They'll help me remove the barriers that keep me from painting because, when I get into the process, it will be very intuitive. But they're just super stressing the painting isn't for anyone. "You're not selling it! You're not even hanging it up! It's the process." (Laughs)

V: It's the process. I love that. Such an important message. Such an important message.

N: They're really reinforcing that.

V: Note this on the recording: The process, not the product.

N: It's very healing. And I can make ugly things, too. They want me to make ugly things. It doesn't have to be pretty. 'Cause again, I'm looking for the purpose, right? They're like, "Mix yellow and green and brown, and put some orange. Make it really ugly!"

V: Yes, why not? Enjoy the process.

N: My ear popped...

V: Okay, I'd like to ask the ancestors if there's anything else that they would like for Natalie to know today or are they done for this moment? They can come in at any time they choose. They're welcome.

N: I saw a young Jim. That's my grandpa's name. He's young, and he is very scrawny. I think he wants to show me something about his life.

V: Okay. Let's allow that to come into view. Allowing young Jim to show Natalie something important today.

N: My grandpa, Jim, is like the best person I've ever known. Like the kind of person you aspire to be. And I feel like he's showing me him, young, around my age. And how he did soften into being that person that I admire over time. He's impressing on me his lesson not to take life so seriously. Almost like he's just chiming in with his own story.

V: Yes. What else does he want you to know?

N: He's showing me himself before he met my grandma… and saying how, when he met her, he crossed into that calmer phase. And that when I move into that phase with my [future] partner, I'll be much more gentle and calm. Not trying to prove myself or prove anything.
  Just be a healing presence more than a doer. And people will be healed by just my presence. When I'm so hardworking, it actually kind of doesn't help people because they think they need to work harder to achieve what I've achieved.
  So, not only will it help me, but I'll help so many other people way more effectively than working on the computer all the time and doing all the things.
  (Pauses) He's smiling. "You got it."

V: Wonderful. There's a lot of wisdom in those words.

N: Yeah, it's powerful. He said he'll be there with me. I'm learning to unravel and let it be easy.

V: Okay. Is there anything else that he would like you to know?

N: I'm gonna get there. It seems like a big change for me [to work less].

(Laughs) They said I'll be carried.

"Let your words heal." And it's not even what I say. It's the codes in my voice. The way I say it. My feeling. So, I don't need to over-strategize what I'm gonna say.

They said, "Just show up and share whatever." 'Cause it could seem pointless to me, but people feel held even if we don't talk about the most goal-oriented or groundbreaking spiritual discovery. Just being there... the presence... the presence and the vibration. Even if I wanna show up at a regular time or not.

No striving. No more striving. You've already done it.

V: They must be very proud.

N: Yeah. They're even more proud of the lessons I'm learning, though. They know how I've been. It's like a miracle.

V: They have lived the human life. They understand.

N: Yeah. There's no judgment. It's kind of like... funny. Because they know I know. I'm fully aware. They're just like, "It's time."

It doesn't matter if I'm well known because the people who need to be touched by me will find me. And they're all on their own journeys, so I don't need to make sure they have their breakthrough.

They want me to paint with my left hand.

V: With your left hand?

N: Yeah. Because I'm not gonna be good at it. (Laughs)

V: I love that. It's not about being good at it. I love that.

N: They're like, "Stomp that out." Being good at things. They said,

"At least in the beginning." 'Cause it's gonna be hard for you not to make it perfect.

V: Yes. What an amazing suggestion. It enhances the process of enjoying the journey and relearning.

N: They're showing me painting with my toes. (Laughs) Oh, they just want me to be really free with it! Like paint with whatever you want. This must be a really big lesson because they're just harping on.

V: Yes. They're hitting it home.

N: They just keep reminding me... "It's not for anybody!"

V: And these are gonna be beautiful lessons you'll be able to pass along as well.

N: Yes. Because of the presence it will create in me. To know that, yeah, my voice is enough. It's a really big relief. I've been working so hard for so long. (Crying)

V: Yes, yes. What a beautiful message that you can relieve yourself of that... that stress. Yeah.

N: I feel a big sense of trust that my income isn't dependent on me working hard.

V: Yes. We can let go of that programming.

N: Yeah. So many people need to learn this.

V: There's such an important lesson that you will be able to communicate to heal people with that lesson. Because that is a construct. It's not a reality.

N: It's keeping so many people stuck. Especially me, so they want me to be like the ambassador.

V: You will be an ambassador of that.

N: If I can do it, anybody can.

V: You will be able to rewire people and reeducate people on the power of joy.

N: And realize they will be... they'll have enough. They'll be *more* abundant. And it doesn't make any sense to our brains.
 And I feel the way I'm speaking feels very clear right now. (Takes a deep breath) Like my Higher Self is saying this.

V: Yes. I'd love to ask the ancestors if this is time for us to communicate with the Higher Self?

N: It's already here. It's very bright and clear. And these acts will allow me to merge with my Higher Self.

Although the Higher Self has been showing me these visions and facilitating this conversation the entire time, it is usually necessary for the practitioner to guide the client out from behind the lens of the prior personalities to communicate with the Higher Self directly.
 In the hypnosis script, there is a suggestion to leave the previously seen past lives behind and let those personalities continue on their

journey. This allows the client to stop seeing things from their past lives' limited perspective and instead tap into the infinite wisdom of the Higher Self, where even greater answers can be found.

V: While we talk to the Higher Self, I want all of the ancestors to know that they are very welcome to participate in this conversation.

N: They're all sitting in a room, having tea.

V: Yes. (Laughs) They can have tea and participate in any way that they see fit. And I want them to know that they are so welcome here. And we're so grateful for all the lessons that they are imparting today.

And at this time I would like to speak to Natalie's Higher Self, please. May I speak to Natalie's Higher Self? Do I have permission to speak to Natalie's Higher Self?

N: Only a little. (Surprised by answer)
I won't be able to answer all the questions.

V: And why is that?

N: I'm a channel and I can find them for myself.

V: Okay, well, I know that Natalie will really appreciate any and all information that is brought forward today.

I know the Higher Self could have brought forward many different lifetimes for Natalie to see today, but we chose to bring forward a select few. What was the purpose of bringing through the first life we viewed of the man who lived in the snowy landscape who worked so hard for his family? What was the purpose of bringing forward that life for her to view?

N: We want her to surrender and find meaning in the moment. Not in her mental construct of what she thinks must be done as a duty. The joy is there. It's always there. We push it away. We think it away. It's a lie.

V: Okay. So, is it a choice for us?

N: It's hard for us. But yes.

V: So, being more present in the moment is important?

N: Use your feelings. Not your mind. It's a disconnected self and it causes a lot of people pain. And then they wanna push away their emotions even more because they don't want to feel the pain that they created in their minds.

V: So, is it recommended for us and other people to feel the pain but move through it?

N: Yes. It is only fleeting. It has a purpose. It's the more direct route.

V: Okay. And I know you brought forward this second life that we viewed of the woman who we first saw in her later life being very independent. What was the purpose of bringing forward that life for her to view?

N: Let love in. Love's purpose is love. Not to get you somewhere. Now you know how to give, let yourself receive. Let others feel the joy of giving because you remember how much joy it brought you. Don't deny them. Be a receiver... of ideas and information... and yes, love.

V: How do we process *not* receiving love?

N: Acceptance. It's not about you. It's a lesson or not the right time, not the right person, not the right conveyor [of love]. It is still there, though. It's just that the love comes forward in a way that may not feel like it's love. The action of turning you away from it is also love. To make space for bigger, better things. Don't dwell on a speck of love when you can have the whole ocean.

V: I love that. Thank you.

N: Don't scrounge for the specks. There's endless [love]. And it's worth the wait.

V: Did she plan to spend a lot of time alone in this lifetime? And if so, what's the reason?

N: Yes. It's only for now. She's learning to come home to herself.

V: Will there be a time in the future where a perfect partner will be in her life?

N: Yes, but even then there will be times of being alone. She'll know how to deal with it. It's not a bad thing to be alone. All one, the word is "all one". It's a beautiful thing because it's an endless sea. An endless source. It's not those specks. It's the ocean.

V: Thank you. I love that analogy.

N: It's the road home.

V: She had a question also about Kabbalah. Does she have a past life connection to Kabbalah or what do you want her to know about that?

N: It's inherent in the fabric of the universe. And she's learning about the universe. It's the symbols that will make it easier for her to understand. Even if it seems complicated, it's a road to understanding. She gets it more than she thinks. And it's not about the mental construct of understanding it. It's the… "feeling" is not a good enough word, but that would be the best word.

V: Is "essence" a word?

N: Yeah, but even that doesn't encompass it. It is an "experience" could be another word. It's a very immersive experience.

It's not about the past lives. It's about the connections that are being made in the present.

V: I'd like to touch upon some questions that she had about her health and her body. She wanted to talk about the spiritual source of her scalp rash. What is the source of that?

N: She wanted to have a bodily issue that needed maintaining. So, when it was out of balance, she would know it's time to nourish herself more… nurture. It will flare up when she's not taking care of herself. It will eventually heal once she learns to make it a way of life.

V: What are some of the things that she can do to help balance her body?

N: Nutrition. Nutrition, nutrition, nutrition.

V: And are there particular aspects of nutrition that you want her to incorporate?

N: It's a way of giving love to the self. And it may feel difficult because I'm learning to give love to myself. It's just a symbolic measure.

V: Does what she's inputting into her body matter, too, for that nutrition and balance? (Yes.)

Do you have certain recommendations on what that should be?

N: Greens. No greasy food. Sometimes it's okay. Whole foods. Take the time to cook. It's not even so much about—yes, it's important what you put in your body—but like with the painting, it's picking the right pot. It's boiling the water. It's being in the moment of the process of nourishment that feels hard because we think we have so much to do, that's more important, that cannot wait, especially in relation to helping others. This is her time to help herself.

V: So, make it a very mindful process?

N: Yes, a ritual. And it will get easier over time. It just feels hard because it's a breakthrough.

Don't go for the easy meals. Make it an art, a masterpiece. Like you're putting together a song and you're fine-tuning the spices from each time you make it to the next. And using pure ingredients sourced from the best places, really putting so much love into every part of the process like she did in the violin life, but now it's focused on providing for herself.

V: Love that. Thank you. She also had a question about the females in her family having their hair fall out.

N: Lack of nourishment.

V: Is it related to the answer of the previous question? Is it about nourishment or is it about anything else?

N: Not to get your sense of self-worth from vanity. Yes, you have to spend more time taking care of your hair, which is a process of nourishment, but it's not about the beauty of how you look. The purpose of the nourishment isn't for beauty.

And all of these women have denied themselves, or they have asked for obstacles, to keep them from fully nourishing themselves. Again, it's that idea of learning through difficulty.

We don't want the nourishment to have an outcome, like a measured outcome of like, "Oh, now I'll be beautiful." We want you to [nourish yourself] because it makes you feel good.

V: Is it another example of enjoying the process?

N: It's enjoying it for the right reasons. Not for where it might bring you, but for how you feel in the moment.

[The hair loss] can also be reversed when the lesson is learned. But she may find that she does not even need it to be reversed because she feels so good just being who she is that it no longer matters. So, don't worry if it happens or when it happens.

V: So, for Natalie, is this something that can be healed?

N: To an extent. It can get better through the nourishment and the greens. So, there will be an outward change, but we want [her] to learn the lesson before it comes to that point, so that it's not because of the outcome.

V: Okay. I know that you have access to all infinite power and healing abilities, and I know that there is this process of learning a lesson in this issue that she talks about with her hair. But can we do some healing on that today?

N: She knows what she needs to do now. She has to do it. She is a healer. She's her best healer.

V: Got it. Thank you.

N: We don't wanna do it for her. It would take away... it would take away the point.

V: Understood. Thank you. She also had a question about the popping in her ears. Can you tell me about the popping in the ears?

N: It's not for her to know now. Trust. She knows. She knows. It's okay.

V: So, is there anything physically wrong with her ears that she needs to be concerned with?

N: Absolutely not. It's part of a process of her receiving from the universe and helping her anchor it into her physical experience.

V: Okay. She also has a question about her relationship with food, having an aversion to food and eating on a regular basis. What would you like her to know about that?

N: It's an aversion to the process of cooking and nourishing, not to the food itself. This is why we've been sending her wrong [takeout] orders., because we want her to not get satisfaction from people doing it for her. The time has come. The time has come.

V: So, this process seems very related to what we talked about with the scalp issue about the process of nourishment to make it a ritual and to make it an art and masterpiece. Is this all connected?

N: Yes, because she will be drawn to the foods that make her feel the best the more she stays with the process and turns it into an art. And she will feel better and look better in many ways. And people will notice.

V: And she'll have a lot to teach to people, won't she?

N: Being a living embodiment of her work. Not someone who spouts out advice. Not someone who speaks of miracles, but one who lives them.

V: Beautiful. I love that. What would you like her to know about her spirit guides?

N: We are working on your behalf at all times. You will come to know us better down the line, and you will come to know that you have always known. It is the process of forgetting that makes the connection stronger when you feel that affinity. We are always here. They are always here. She is one. To others. To herself.

V: Yes, wonderful. She also had a question of why she has felt so drawn to living in Hawaii. What's her connection to Hawaii?

N: This is her healing place where she's going just for herself. Not for anyone else, but for her own joy. It's not about what she's showing other people is even possible, although sometimes that might be what she thinks. It's really for her own nourishment, and to learn… to learn her lessons through joy and beauty. And surrendering to the miracles around, which are much more easy to see here. They're more embodied here.

There are many connections to this land. Some she may come to discover in time, but that is the past. It's more about the healing that can happen in the present, and the actions that must be taken to do so.

V: She's talked about wanting to potentially move to Maui at some point.

What would you like her to know about that?

N: She needs to open up to receive—to earn—the money… "earn" isn't the word… the money that is needed will come when she surrenders. She will have everything she dreams of and more when she learns to let go of being the one responsible for taking every little step to make things happen. It is the allowing that must happen now, and receiving help. She does not need to do it herself. She will not do it herself.

V: That was also a life lesson in one of her lives, wasn't it?

N: She will be very resistant to this, but it will give her what she wants.

V: Okay. She also had a question about why she's so fascinated and obsessed with space.

N: She lives in space. Even now this is only one aspect of her being here. She never left. This is an experiment or a construct to bring back knowledge on this experience that humans go through, but she never left. She will be with us more fully in the future. It may seem like a long time, but it's really not.

V: Yes. What cosmic races is she most tied to?

N: Pleiadian. But at the moment she can relate more to Arcturian. So, we have been teaching her about that because she can relate to the more analytical structuring. The Pleiadian aspect of her is yet to be further awakened. It's a more feminine side. It's not about giving up the other side. It's about integrating.

V: That makes sense. Thank you.

*Note: Pleiadian starseeds are those souls who are said to have come from the

Pleiades star cluster, located in the constellation of Taurus. Arcturians are known as a very advanced extraterrestrial civilization from Arcturus, the brightest star located in the Boötes constellation close to the Virgo constellation.

V: She wanted to have some insight into why astrology is so easy for her.

N: It's her connection to the stars, and she's bringing it down as a bridge. It's so old. It's been there for so long. It's a sign of her remembering... re-membering... and coming closer to her source. So, it's been there, but now it has come to the surface of her experience to be shared and to teach. And in that process, she's remembering more herself.

V: Did she ever have past lives where astrology was a part of what she did?

N: Yes. But it wasn't always in a healing sense. Sometimes it was to gain power or help others gain power, and that did not sit right with her. So, she wanted to use it to heal, and to go to the higher levels of what it's meant to be used for.

V: And is that what she's doing in this lifetime?

N: She's only scratching the surface. But there's so much more to come. And it's not about the mental connection to it. It's what we want to always get across. It's the feeling... the essence... but there's a higher octave of that word that can't be brought across. We're moving her out of the mental, into the experiential.

V: Okay. Beautiful. She also wanted to know... are there things that she can do to strengthen her channeling?

N: Nourish. All the steps that have been provided. We are always here. As she opens up to receive herself more, she will open up to receive us more.

V: She also had a question of why did she get sick when she got sick? What was the reason for that?

N: Many times she has gotten sick to slow herself down and let the calendar go - and to realize it wasn't even that important to begin with. Other times, she has become sick to visit with us, to spend more time in the astral plane than she does on Earth, to learn lessons here and have conversations about how to proceed.

V: What is the best way for her to strengthen her path going forward?

N: It's in the unraveling of the "used to"... of the "used to be". It has carried her to where she is now, but now she gets to explore more.

Note: I was not only beginning to work less, but I was also moving away from being an astrologer, which was mental work that was very focused on calendars and planning using very small, specific details.

V: You talked about her receiving her own love. Can we talk a little bit more about that? (Yes.)
   Would you like her to know about receiving her own love? Are we talking about self-love? What do you want her to know about receiving her own love?

N: She does love herself on one level, but it doesn't always reflect in the day-to-day actions because she's very up in her head and scattered.
   She thinks she will help more people and give more love by doing more, working harder, because that is what she knows. Because in the past that's how she got love. How she gave love.

We want her to learn through receiving. It doesn't have to be hard. It's going to be easy! She just thinks it's hard.

V: If you were to give her an example of something she could do… let's say, on a daily basis… to remind herself of that or to help initiate that receiving of love, what would that be?

N: Meditating with her hand on her heart. Giving herself Reiki. Don't be afraid to look in the mirror. Witness yourself. And make your day about food, even if it takes many steps. You won't be able to receive the love of your soulmate until you can receive your own.

V: I know we have a beautiful connection with the Higher Self right now. What else do you want her to know? I'm sure there's many things you would like her to know.

N: She will know when she's going in the wrong direction because it hurts or it feels stressful. Follow the path of ease. The current will take you. The current is flowing. We don't even need to steer.

V: I love that. Do us humans make this all too complicated?

N: We must.

V: Why do humans make this complicated?

N: It's a process of unlearning. What worked in the past is not what will work in the future. Just because you master one lesson doesn't mean it's appropriate to take that same method in future circumstances. Be adaptable. There is no end to learning. Don't act like you have mastered it. It doesn't mean that life gets easier when you master something, because there will be something more to master.

V: I know this may be a hard question, but what are some of the most important lessons that an Ascended Master has learned from being a human?

N: Honor thyself. You are the vehicle for transformation of yourself and then others.

V: I know that her ancestors brought forward some beautiful information about joy. What do you want her to know about joy... the importance of joy?

N: It is everything. That's all there is. Surrender to the path before you. You have been given the steps. Honor thyself.

V: What are the best things for Natalie or any human to do when we become fearful?

N: Feel the fear. Embrace it. It's where your blocks lie.

V: How is it most recommended to work through the fear? I know there's different methods out there.

N: Look at it. Don't obsess over it. Question it. Why is it there? What is it teaching you? What if you didn't have it? What could you do? What is it keeping you from doing? All of life is a series of facing fears to unravel the great mysteries. It's a tool. Fear is nothing to fear. It just is. It will never be eliminated completely.

V: Is there an existence where there is no fear?

N: Yes, but Natalie doesn't have that access yet. "It's above her pay grade,"

I'm hearing. (Both laugh)

V: Is there anything you'd like her to know with regards to her career, her work? I know she's doing an amazing job, and we got some suggestions about that. Anything else you'd like her to know?

N: Trust. She doesn't need to know more than that. She's doing great. She's doing better than she thinks.

V: Would this be a good time to do a body scan for her?

N: It's almost time to end.

V: Would it be all right for us to bring in some healing today for her body or rejuvenation and maybe some balancing? (Okay.)
 I'd like for the Higher Self to bring in that healing, and balancing, and harmony into her body at this time. I know the Higher Self knows way more about that than me and is in charge here today. So, please feel free to describe to me what it is that you're bringing into her body to provide her some relief and healing and balancing at this time. And just let me know when you are complete.

N: We are reconnecting her synapses to act as one whole force instead of separate from each other. The healing will continue into tonight, but the biggest part is complete.

V: Thank you. Is there anything else that you would like Natalie to know today? We have this recording that we're making for her. Is there anything that you'd like to put on this recording that is just a really important reminder for her?

N: Embrace the journey. She already knows she's already planned it. Let it carry her. She's in good hands. You can float high above the ethers in your sleep and visit us. We are always here. We are always with you. We have never left. We will never leave. We are complete.

Chapter 3: Awakening to Past Life Wisdom

Not all past lives are basic and boring lives filled with hard work and struggle. We may be surprised to discover that we held deep wisdom or even harnessed special powers in our past lives. Perhaps we lived in fascinating places and time periods or held roles that would seem far more interesting than what we are doing now.

If we remembered this, it may change our perception of ourselves and what we believe we're capable of. We may feel more confident knowing that we have far more experience than we ever realized. From our Higher Self, we may receive the support we need to harness these abilities and make the most of them in our current lifetime.

A year after my first hypnosis session, I began training to become a hypnosis practitioner myself. I wanted to continue exploring the nature of the Higher Self and witness firsthand how it worked. Training for this was a challenging process that expanded my beliefs immensely. I had to take many breaks to process what I was learning because it felt like getting psychic brain surgery as my mindset stretched with each lesson. I often joked that QHHT® *(Quantum Healing Hypnosis Technique)* training was like a spiritual awakening in a box. After my graduation, A was one of the first clients I worked with in person.

A's extraordinary experience illustrates a time and place when she was a respected healer in her community with strong, intuitive abilities that are not typically well-known or celebrated in modern times. Because she was hoping to transition into doing more of this type of work in her current life, A's past life in an ancient civilization was a reminder that she already holds the capability for facilitating healing to a degree she may not have ever considered before.

N: Tell me the very first thing that you see or the very first impressions that you have.

A: It looks like red sand. And little sprouts of grass. Everything is red because of the stone. It's Mesopotamia, and there are people with tan, brown skin, and the whites of their eyes are so white.

N: Is there anything in the distance?

A: There are temples that look kind of like pyramids. The colors are so rich. The blues are so deep, and the golds are so vibrant.

N: Beautiful. What else is around you?

A: Their lights are like fire. So, it's like these torches are lining the walkways. Everyone just feels so present and happy in this market or square that I'm in, with the temples in the backdrop.

N: How do you feel in this place?

A: Natural. It's like people look at me, but I don't stand out. I look like them, and I'm just there watching everyone, observing what they're doing, just seeing how they live.

N: What are they doing?

A: I see moms walking around holding their children's hands, and they're giggling. I see people playing with these balls. I see a lot of people smiling and laughing. It's like everything is so simple and so present. People are just here, and they're happy to be here, and I can hear music playing in the background. It just feels like everyone is so joyful, and it's like this undercurrent of feeling held. Everyone is just held and supported.

N: Are you standing in place, or are you doing something?

A: I'm standing in place on these wooden planks. It's kind of like a boardwalk, but it's on the ground, and it's wooden, and all of these boardwalks lead throughout the market and the square to the temples. That is where... it's just so sacred and healing.

N: All roads lead to the temple.
    If you look down at your feet, what do you see?

A: I have tan feet, and I'm wearing sandals. They're really, really thin sandals. It's kind of like you wear them just to protect your feet from the burning sand or the boardwalk.

N: No support. (Right.)
    What are you wearing on your body?

A: It's like a sarong type of thing. It's black and white.

N: Do you have any jewelry or ornaments on your body?

A: I have a gold anklet. It's like tiny little gold beads on my left ankle. It's in honor of a goddess. It's grounding to wear it. And the gold color is the frequency reminder of the goddess to be the light.

N: Can you make out which goddess?

A: I hear the name Azraelle.

Note: Upon further research, we discovered that Azraelle is the name of the ancient goddess of life, death, and rebirth.

N: Do you have any other jewelry?

A: I have a ring. I have a gold band on my left hand, my ring finger.

N: Are you wearing anything on your head?

A: I think it's just my hair. It's really dark. Black hair. It's long.

N: Does your body feel male or female?

A: It feels like I lean towards female, but it's like a balance of masculine and feminine. It's kind of like I walk through the world, and people don't totally understand me, but I came to be the balance of both. To just be grounded in my knowing I'm there to be that balance.

N: How does your body feel? Does it feel healthy?

A: I'm standing in the sun, and the sun feels so good. I think I'm just meant to observe people and to see what brings them joy, to see what brings them connection, to see how they interact with each other, to see what words they don't say. To see the little things that they communicate in ways that are without words.

N: What do you feel you're meant to learn from observing?

A: How the energy of connection is facilitated between people when there isn't a language. To see how people carry themselves through life to see what presence means when you're with another.

N: Beautiful. Do you live near here? Take me to the place where you live and look at the outside of it. Describe it for me.

A: I live across the river. It's a circular home made out of the red sand and stone together. It's small, but it feels really safe.

N: And how do you go inside of it?

A: You open this door that shuts, but most of the homes around don't have doors. Anyone can just come and go as they please, but I have a door.

N: Why have you chosen to have a door?

A: I need to keep control of who comes in and out of my home because some people want to come, but they don't read the cues for when to leave and I'm tired. But I like having people feel comfortable even if it means I'm exhausted.

N: So, closing the door sends them the message you're not open for visitors? (Yes.)
    Go ahead and go inside and describe the interior.

A: I have a small bed, and I have a little table with candles and incense. It's a small home. There isn't a kitchen, but that's because everyone in the community cooks together, and they bring their own fruits and their own things to dinner or whatever meal, so we support each other. But then your home is your sacred space.

N: Do you live with anyone?

A: I don't think so because the bed is really small and it's like everything is set how exactly I would want it.

N: What do you do with the majority of your time here?

A: I like going on walks. I like connecting with people and hearing their stories. I like listening to the music. I like going to the temples. The temples are healing.

The top of the temple is open to the sky, and people go to receive cosmic energy. I like to go, and I like to think about life and everything beyond that. The temples elevate your frequency in a way where it can take you to new thoughts and new questions to ask yourself that maybe you haven't been aware of.

But I like to go alone. I spend a lot of time alone.

N: Do you have any responsibilities here?

A: It feels like I serve as a guide of some sort. It's like people bring me their questions about their life, and I help them think differently. I help them tell new stories. I help teach them how to learn more about themselves because people are busy.

But I spend so much time alone that it's like I'm accessing different questions to ask because I do that by myself and I'm not distracted.

I think that people get a sense of calm around me. They like to be around me because they feel grounded, they feel safe. And because I'm not distracted because I don't have children, it's like I hold this space for them to just relax a little bit in their life.

N: Beautiful. Is there anything in particular you feel like doing in this place?

A: Down the river, if you walk far enough, there is this secluded waterfall. The water is like turquoise blue, and the sound is amazing! The way the water falls is like music, and you can go there and you can release all of your worries into the waterfall, and allow Earth to take those away from you down the river. I go there because I bring people's worries with me to release them into the river so they don't have to carry the burden anymore.

N: Mmm yes, beautiful. What do you feel like doing next?

A: I like sitting in the sun. It's so warm and peaceful. And listening to the water. It's like I have this communal relationship with the water. It's like this kinship. I am the water, too, so I like to be around her. It's like she gets me. We have an unspoken language. It's like she can take everything from you and give you everything you need to survive.

She's *that* compassionate and generous that she would help you live and take the pain. Most people can't hear her until she's making waves, until there's pain she could bring to you, but she doesn't want to. But sometimes the Earth needs her to move because it's a reminder that we all should be moving and changing because if we're stagnant, things grow that maybe we don't want. Things that could be causing illness or suffering. So, it's a healthy flow.

N: Beautiful. Let's go ahead and leave that scene and let's move forward to an important day, a day that you consider to be important. What's happening? What do you see?

A: It's my birthday, and there's a party happening, and I'm wearing... I have so many bangles and jewels up and down my arms. Everyone is in such a good mood, so joyful. People are hugging each other and smiling and laughing, and it is amazing.

I am looking at everyone thinking, "My God, all of these people are here because they love me." Everyone is just embracing each other and laughing and telling each other stories, and everyone is so present with each other. It's like friends who haven't seen each other in years, and here they are, and it's like I facilitated these connections.

N: Beautiful. It's a happy day! What else is happening around you?

A: I'm just listening to people. I'm seeing people get closer as they talk because more and more voices are talking, so it's like they have to be closer to hear each other.

N: Can you hear what any of them are saying?

A: I'm hearing people... it's like I can't hear exactly word for word what they're saying, but I can hear intuitively the themes.
    So, I hear people connecting over politics in the region. I hear another group talking about agriculture and farming practices. I'm hearing a whole bunch of mothers in a circle talking about parenthood, and I can hear little kids giggling.
    I feel this inner sense or knowing that I had to have this party, not so much to celebrate me, but to create connections with people in person because I'm connected to so many people and see so many themes, but not everyone thinks like me or has the connections. So, bringing them together to meet each other is what was most important so that people could see that they weren't alone, and so they could meet like-minded people like them, so they had a friend or a source they could rely on because I was so trusted.

N: So, it's not just happy for you, but everyone?

A: Yes. Everyone is so happy. Ah! It's joyful, and it's jubilant. Everyone is in such high spirits, and it's kind of like their high energy is raising the frequency of the planet. It's like if more people were connected in joy, it makes the world better.

N: So, it's like a spiritual experience and not just a social gathering!

A: But they don't know that. But I know that.
It's kind of like... in my mind's eye.... I'm seeing these neural networks connect, and when the connections happen, there's a spark of light, and that light moves throughout the network, and that's what I'm seeing with people.
Their energies are sparks and connecting with each other, and it's the joy that's the movement. And it's as if everyone is connecting with open hearts because they're making new friendships, or they're being seen, or they're feeling like I'm not the only one, and it's transcending the human experience and bringing that to higher levels of consciousness because joy is so high and beautiful.

N: You have very strong intuitive abilities!
Beautiful. Let's go ahead and leave that scene and move forward to another important day. Be there now. What's happening?

A: It is night, and I'm back in Mesopotamia, but it's like years in the future, so many years into the future. I'm seeing the temples are kind of in ruins, and the entire place is lit up by the stars, and it's still.
The moon on the temple is incredible, but it's so quiet here. People have forgotten that it exists. And to some, that would be heartbreaking, but to me, it feels peaceful because I don't want people around who can't understand and cherish the temple and what it can bring to people.
But it feels important that it's at night, and it feels important like I'm supposed to see this. It's like even though everything here is so much older, it's still potent. It still carries the same energy even if it looks differently, and it's like I'm hearing this metaphor for aging. That

is why aging is so beautiful - because it's the same energy but different experiences.

Even the sand is cool. It's cold, but it feels so safe even though I'm alone at night in the dark.

N: Is there anything else you're meant to see in this place?

A: It's like looking at—I don't know how to describe it—but there is a symbolism carved in gold in the temple, and the way the moon hits it makes it light up so you can't not look at it.

And it feels like codes for consciousness that, because we're so far into the future of these temples, people can't read or understand, but they feel it on a really deep level. But the codes are what we've always had for consciousness. The codes are just love and remembering your divine nature in your spirit.

N: Do you have any sense of how we forget these codes... besides the ruins becoming old?

A: We forget because we're taught not to listen to ourselves. We're taught that there are certain frequencies that are evil, but evil isn't the right word. Harmful by certain powers of ego because if people were to reach these higher frequencies, they would be free. If they were to integrate these codes, they would be free.

But we want men to be looked at as gods and to forget that we are the gods and the goddesses. But if we have people in power, we give away our sovereignty. If we give away our sovereignty and our free will, we can be controlled.

And it's not that most people in power want to control, but they really only know about fear-based control. They don't understand how much better everything and everyone would be if they held these codes and remembered them, rediscovered them. But people crave power because they crave meaning.

N: To feel like they are meaningful?

A: Yeah. They crave power because they're afraid of death. They're afraid of being so out of control. They're afraid of what could happen if everyone was free and how people would be - not realizing that what the gods and goddesses bring to Earth is the freedom to be the fractals, the essences of God.

N: So, the fear gets in people's way?

A: Yes. But the problem is that the fear is really, really loud and controlling, and it's like the people in power who have been conditioning people to lose their sovereignty and their magic... these people in power, it's like they wear lenses of black. They look through perspectives that are shaded in grays, and it's like it runs through every fiber of their being and every synapse in their brain, thinking that this is what's going to bring them meaning and to leave a legacy, even if they have to use fear, because it's as if the ends justify the means.

They would rather be remembered as powerful and have their name stamped in history than be nameless and nothing at all, but they don't understand that their energetic signature is what will be remembered anyway by those who are meant to, and that the most powerful energetic signatures are the ones laced in love.

It's what our Ascended Masters are remembered for. It wasn't the fear that they unleashed; it was the love that they grew, the love that they planted in each and every heart, the way they walk through the world.

We have all of those opportunities, but the ego says differently, and the temples are important because the temples are about devotion to yourself, to contemplate for yourself what your sovereignty means.

The temples are a time to reflect for you. It's not necessarily about downloading information from the gods. It's about rediscovering from within that voice with the wisdom and the connection to the all that is. And that is why I like going to these temples.

N: Are you here at this temple as a spirit? It's long after the time when you lived.

A: Yes. It's so quiet. It's so beautiful in the moonlight. It's like a hidden treasure, but it's a hidden treasure because it's my treasure. Because in that lifetime, I unlocked secrets of the universe there, but it's because I heard them from within. So, I'm the caretaker of the sanctuary.

N: Amazing. Is there anything else you'd like to explore in this place?

A: When I stand in the temple, and I look up, I can see the stars, and I see this swirling, misty light coming down through the center, and I don't know what it means, but I'm meant to see it. And I may not know what it means for a while, but it was meant for me... like an activation maybe.

N: How are you feeling as this happens?

A: Very curious, but the energy around this swirling light feels beautiful. I'm not scared, and it feels warm and inviting. It's kind of like the light mimics the way DNA helixes look. There's something there genetically for me... like codes of light or rememberings or whisperings of divine thoughts from the past. An awakening of ancient information shared from the stars that took lightyears to get to me. And I'm not meant to know what it is now. I'm just meant to receive with no resistance, just to receive something that was made for me.

N: Let's enjoy this activation for a moment. Take it all in, and let me know when it's complete.

A: It's like even though everything was dark, my entire body became gold, and I watched my really dark hair turn to this really vibrant gold color. I watched my third eye open and become gold, and it's like I'm literally radiating light.

N: Beautiful. And you can carry this with you forward now.

Okay, let's go ahead and drift away from that life. And now may I speak to A's Higher Self please? (Yes.)

I know that the Higher Self could have brought forth many different lifetimes for A to see today. You chose to bring forward the life as the guide in Mesopotamia for her to see. Why did you pick that lifetime to show her?

A: To illustrate the example that this is natural for her and that she's been doing this for lifetimes... to not doubt the alignment of the calling.

N: What were you trying to tell her about her life now?

A: She doubts a lot of her gifts because of what she does so effortlessly, and she looks to other people who have the success that she wants and wonders why not her. It's the reminder to take a breath and to trust that it will be her.

But it's like she's gathering threads of a blanket. She's gathering the threads to create what will be a masterpiece, and needs to trust the process. Every person she holds space for or guides is a part of the thread of that masterpiece, and each are important. She's gathering and needs to feel certain and confident in what she is weaving.

N: Yes, it's like the connections that were being made as she watched the party and the people coming together. Amazing. Is there anything else you wanted to show her through sharing that life?

A: She forgets that what is effortless for her is not for another, and she takes it for granted and doubts. The key is in releasing the doubt, and owning that connection is the key that will elevate humanity.

Because the world is so siloed, and they believe that borders are what's going to keep them safe and separate them, but it's our human connection to our human evolution. And each of us holds a key, and each of us holds a lock. And when the right keys are turned in the right locks, everything can change for the better.

So, trusting that the connections she's making are divine, and to trust the people that she meets, and to trust the journey and the process.

One cannot weave an entire tapestry in a single day with millions of threads. [The message is] to relax and be patient and present to the words that people are saying and the things that people are experiencing… so that she can create connections to those people… so that they can find each other and remember who they are and what they bring to the planet.

Because at the highest level, seeing this tapestry and the way that it moves in the world and all of the little stories and all of the little beams of light that make up each and every thread is truly a sight to behold. And the universe is better because of this tapestry that we make up.

Everyone is in awe of how beautiful the human experience is because even if it's painful or hard, the love is immeasurable. They just have to remember it. They just have to see it and choose it every time.

N: Yes, and it's worth the wait for all the threads coming together, isn't it?

A: It's worth the wait.

N: What is A's soul mission?

A: In a metaphoric way, it's to burn as bright as fire and to remember that not everyone likes fire. Some are actually burned by it, but it is no reason to not burn. What she knows is true, and maybe some people need to be burned by the fire to realize who they are and what they stand for.

And every person has an ember inside of them that, with enough oxygen and care, can turn into beautiful blazes of light, but there's always an ember that starts it. There are people like her on the planet right now who have flames and who are burning, and they're gifting their fire to others who are ready, but not everyone is ready and that is okay.

N: Yes, she's a firestarter. Anything else?

A: When I look at her, it's like she's opening doors to people's hearts, and she wants to do that with everyone, but she keeps her heart pretty closed. This is the nudge to just open the door and to trust that even those with closed hearts can't harm her. Because a lot of people are closed right now - not understanding how Spirit moves in and out through your heart and how connections are made through the heart.

There's a language that people speak without words, through the heart, that they resonate with. And even if everyone isn't ready for that level of love, a few people have to be, and it's safe no matter what. It's safe no matter what.

N: Yes, it's just an illusion that it isn't safe.

A: The human experience and belief structures make you believe it isn't. But beliefs hold on because they have to. That's their one job. Because if you don't believe it, where does it go? And if you do believe it, you anchor it and materialize it in your reality. And if everything is an illusion, what would we see if we didn't have things that anchored us into reality? Things like fear and doubt and overwhelm and suffering... it adds to the richness and the depth of the human experience.

N: Yes. Why is this soul mission so important for A?

A: She's restless. There's this recurring theme of, "What is it like when things aren't perfect?" It's one thing to be in the heavens by Source, and to experience good and perfect and well. But she wants color. It's like she wants to be the prism, a vessel of light that expands the fractals of the human experience to showcase what you can do with a single beam of light. And she wants to experience those colors.

When you're in the heavens or beyond in the spiritual realm, things are beautiful because they just are. But what if you created the beauty yourself? What if you made the meaning? What if you transmuted any color or anything you didn't like and made it something beautiful because you could?

And that is why the Creator created us to create, to experience that level of love, a level of love so deep that you would be allowed to create like the Creator. Because the Creator wants us to experience the joy of creation, even if that means experiencing sadness and depression and despair and grief, but it's still creation, creating on this endless, infinite loop. To be so loved so fully that you, too, got to create. How divine is that?

N: Would you say that it's the darkness and the suffering that gives us ideas on what we want to create as well?

A: It's like it's the contrast. How would you know what you truly wanted if you weren't willing to sit on the opposite end... if you weren't willing to sit in the shadows and to experience the richness of the shadows?

N: Yeah, they can be beautiful, too, can't they?

A: We wouldn't judge a leaf on its shade of green. We love it no matter what, but humans think that just because something is dark and dense and heavy, it's not beautiful. It's just a different shade of experience.

N: Yes. That's something we've been learning racially on this planet as well.

A: We have different races so that we can open our hearts to different beings as they come and as we evolve. If everyone looked like us, people who didn't wouldn't be safe to our bodies and to our brains because our brains are wired for safety, which is why celebrating diversity is key.
Because if we can start with people who look like us but maybe a little bit different, maybe we can start welcoming in other species who don't necessarily look like us, but they have the highest intentions for our planet.

N: And can even bring us the help we've been looking for, which we can't receive if we're scared? (Right.)

A: It's a different frequency. Like a different radio station playing.

N: How's A doing with her soul mission so far?

A: She leans pretty hard on herself because there's this drive to push through, to race against the clock, but she doesn't realize it's not in the pushing. It's in the being. But it's not necessarily just about the being… it's about the knowing, and the knowing of just existing is the gift.
But it's because we also come here to experience as much as possible on core themes that pushes her to the brink sometimes to her detriment, but it's the intention to experience… where if she would just release her grip and relax, everything will click into place the way it's meant to. You can't control destiny when it's already been written, so why not relax and trust?

N: Yes. A's wondering which direction she should take with her business offerings. What can you share about that?

A: All roads lead to home. She believes that they're all different paths, but no matter which way you walk, it's forward, it's home.

The better question would be... what would she create if there was no pressure? What would she offer if she trusted in herself and knew the right people would find it instead of the pressure to create for the masses?

And not tying the outcome to a financial goal, but tying the outcome to certainty in her soul and the feeling that every offering is divinely gifted.

Remove any ideas or beliefs around what is deemed successful versus what is deemed impactful, and remember that not everyone has the calling that she believes and surrounds herself with. Every person is unique in the tapestry. Again, every offering is unique at the right time.

So, what would she create without pressure and with a sense of play and curiosity, knowing anything and everything can be shifted along the way? Removing the pressure is the key.

N: Yes. So, the best direction is whichever one feels the lightest.

A: The lightest and what feels like a step forward towards curiosity, light, levity, joy, play. It feels like a whispering and to release the attachment to any outcome of it having to serve her in some way.

N: Yes. So, creating to create. Not necessarily for it to take her somewhere in particular. And how will that help her to approach her business in that way?

A: What I'm seeing is a book, and she wants the book to be a certain offer written in one way. She doesn't realize the offer, and every offer, is a chapter in the larger book of her life. And so she needs to trust that what she's given is meant to be written.

And the book that she'll read from when she's back home will be filled with wisdom and adventures and tales. Everything is drawing in together in and of itself, and it is perfect, but she'll always be writing [the book]. And that is important to know because every chapter changes. Because if they didn't, how boring of a book that would be?

N: She'll be writing her future, you mean? (Yes.)
Can she choose whatever she wants to write?

A: She can, and it's been predestined. What's happening is there's a convergence of desires and timelines, and it's confusing and causing mental blocks or narratives or beliefs.

It's not about converging timelines... it's about seeing each timeline for what it is. It's about trusting again that no timeline is wrong if all timelines lead home.

N: (Remembering the visions from earlier) All paths lead to the temple.

A: All paths lead to the temple. (Smiles)
And the temple is home, and the temple is you, and your heart and your soul.

N: That's beautiful. How can A become less stressed about time?

A: To stop focusing on it as a material thing and to remember it's only but a guideline. You can warp time and shape it in a certain way, and you are not bound by three-dimensional reality focused on time-space.

In higher frequencies, time is malleable, much more malleable. But living and breathing in an aging body and an ego that tells you you're tied to time is the story to rewrite. Know that by working with belief structures, you can heal yourself. By working with your thoughts, you can heal yourself.

Who then is bound by time when they're eternal? Why not play with the malleability of time and relax into it instead of feeling constricted and bound by it?

N: Yes. So, when A's getting off work each day, what would be the highest path for her to do with her time... that she senses as being limited at times?

A: To lay flat on the ground or on the bed, to turn off the screens, and to just breathe in presence to her body. To lose herself in the spaciousness of not being bound by time after the workday, and to just be for a moment for herself. Creating that temple if only for a moment, gathering her energy and every breath.

N: And how will that help her?

A: Closing the door mentally to the job helps her open another door to possibility, and that's important. The peacefulness of just being - where no one needs anything from her - that's important because the world will always need something from you when they're not living within. The world will unravel our threads if you allow yourself to be frazzled by external reality. But when you give yourself a moment to be with yourself, and you breathe into your body, your temple, and you open up, the guidance will be received in the way it is most needed.

N: Beautiful. How can A heal her feeling of scarcity around money?

A: To remember the waterfall in the river, and the flow. To remember that everything is abundant if you choose it. Everything is prosperous if you choose it. To look at money as a multi-layered, multi-dimensional energy that presents itself in many different ways, even outside of it being a tangible object or an electronic object. It's in so many beautiful things that make up physical reality. And it's to appreciate the generosity of Mother Earth and the generosity of creation.

Look at that frequency of money as multi-layered and not just a single string that the world focuses too heavily on. Remember that currency flows in the current of creation and currency. Could be gold, could be paper, money could be an electronic number on your digital screen. The currency will always flow as it's meant to.

So, to expand the awareness of what currency is and how it presents itself, knowing we're all supported as creation. So, what do you wish to create, and how will you receive that currency?

N: What about A's fear that success won't last even if she does attain it again through her own work?

A: It's laughable because success is inherent as a spirit on Earth because you are already successful for being born. How could you not be... to be so brave and courageous to experience density to the depth that humans do?

It's not about "Will I be successful?" It's "How will I celebrate being a success, being born a success?" It's not about "Will I be successful or will it not last?" It's "We are all love, and that is inherently successful as the language of the universe. We are already successful because we are love." What's outside of that? The ego.

The ego will do anything in its power to make you believe anything that you've tasked it to. If you've tasked it to show you success and that it doesn't last, you'll only experience more of it. It is the frame of what is the opposite of experiencing something that doesn't last. It's eternity, infinity, it's infallible energy.

Who is not successful then? And what is the term "last" in human language, when everything is infinite? We just believe it doesn't last because we chose a physical density to experience aging and to experience loss. But even loss is successful because loss is going back home.

N: So, it's not a bad thing if it doesn't last or if it does?

A: It's the meaning you make of it. So, how can you make it mean something loving always and in all ways?

N: Yes. Beautiful. So, she doesn't need to worry about that? (No need.)

N: What about A's family? Why did she choose to be born into this family?

A: To experience pain and to choose love. To be the wise guide for the family system, to serve as a pinnacle for others in her lineage, to choose something different. Even if there was suffering and pain, to experience density in a way that even if it is the darkest, deepest experience, every single person has the choice to choose the light and to showcase to the world what it means to live through pain and to feel gratitude for it because of where you can go from that pain and from that darkness if you decide it.

And this is a particularly prominent time on the planet because it is shrouded in darkness, and everyone has pain and suffering, but who is willing to choose the opposite? And that is why connections are important because the more lights that connect with more lights, the brighter love becomes.

N: Yes. So, it was priming her for her future, but it also allowed her to use her gifts from the past.

A: Yes. [The lesson is] also to choose love even if someone is abusive, even if people cannot meet your needs... to be so generous with your love because that is what God would do. That is what Jesus would do to be the embodiment of forgiveness, and generosity, and love, because of the way that frequency is on the planet.

We are all just walking frequencies trying to find our radio stations, and the only way we find each other is by being that vibration.

N: Yes, and being the vibration of what you want to experience, too, helps you experience more of that.

A: It's like an amplification of the sound that's heard through the stars.

Note: I occasionally offered to ask questions about clients' astrology charts in the sessions. Being a former professional astrologer, I was curious about the connection between our astrology charts and what our Higher Selves planned for us in this lifetime.

N: Why did A choose to have her Moon Sign in Virgo in this lifetime?

A: To learn to decipher the intuitive voice versus the ego's voice. Because the ego's voice is loud and noisy and chaotic and will drop your feelings into such a state where you feel overwhelmed or helpless or out of control when that's not true, and it is to choose the opposite.

It's like unwinding the cords in a ball of knots. Do you want to spend your time unraveling those cords and listening to those thoughts, or do you want to take a step back and breathe into the most loving thought, the lightest thought?

Knowing that all of those cords could be in hues of grays or (whispers) black, but it's that loving thought that's gold... that helps you sidestep the chaos. But she would not have found that if not to wade through the thickness of the thoughts that tell her anything other than love.

N: So, her Moon Sign takes her through the process to help her learn what she's meant to learn. What was the process like for her in choosing to have her astrology chart be the way it is?

A: The process is the map. There are codes in the map that she wanted to experience, and those codes are beautiful in meaning and purpose, but may not be experienced as beautiful and that is okay. It is not to judge those points. It is to receive the wisdom of them.

N: So, are there points on her chart she did not choose and just has to experience?

A: Everyone has those. You have to have them. Otherwise, again, how boring would the adventure be if you knew every single point... when surprises add richness and texture to your story?

N: Yes. Beautiful. What's a gift A has that she's not seeing because it's too close to her?

A: She can hear codes in water. There are stories written in the drops of water that make up the world. There's this feeling that putting her hands and her feet in the water can bring her wisdom, but actually taking time to do that is what is important.

N: Yes, because we bathe every day, but it's not always a conscious communion. And what will that bring to her life if she spends more time connecting with water?

A: She will have clarity on her own true thoughts and not the thoughts that are bound in knots. Not the chaos, the anxiety, or the confusion. It's the water that clears the slate. But taking time to clear the slate requires consciousness and intention in a world that tells you to be busy and to distract yourself... when there's so much water wants to share.
   There's so much to learn, and people forget how much moves within

them as beings of water and matter. To physically exist as matter itself with water flowing within you - making up structures in your body, crystallizing thoughts, ideas, and beliefs, allowing it to flow and break apart. When you do clear and cleanse, there's so much we can learn from water, so much we can shift and change in our states as she (water) does.

N: Yes. So, it's a very powerful gift that she can be harnessing more of.

How can A lessen the pressure of commitment in her beautiful relationship?

A: To face the fear of what it would mean if she were alone with herself. Being in relation with another is beautiful, but sitting with yourself when no one is around is another thing. It's easy to leave relationships, but it's hard to leave yourself. Facing the fear of what it would mean to be alone will unlock wisdom and lighten the load she carries.

It's also in rewriting the stories, knowing that how other people live does not mean that is the case for you. Many people go into marriages and relationships in order to grow. But they're not always meant to be with that person, so they make the story mean something. They darken it, dampen it, belittle it. Tell the world to torch marriages down. They add this edginess to a marriage when really what it is is just a dance. And some people dance with one person for their whole life, and some people dance with multiple partners, and all of it is beautiful... all of it is growth.

N: She spent a lot of time alone in the life you showed her, and she was happy because she wasn't really alone. There were other people around, of course.

What about A's apartment and how it has been feeling a little less than ideal? How can she manifest her dream home?

A: There's no need to manifest when it's already on the timeline. It's relaxing into the presence of your daily life, knowing and trusting that it's already on its way.

And to relax, to focus on lowering stress. Because the stress and anxiety is heightening the loud sounds she hears, and she hyper-focuses on it, and spins into a downward spiral. If she took more time to relax, to release stress, more things wouldn't bother her. She would breathe a little bit lighter. To trust, to surrender, and relax.

N: Yes. So, the things she doesn't like about [her apartment], like the loud noises, are teaching her?

A: They're showing her more of where her stress is. The quicker the stress, the louder it is to relax. It's amplifying and showing her how much pressure and control she's gripped to.

N: Yes, that's a powerful lesson. How will learning this lesson help her in the future?

A: To know that no one is ever in control in the human body. We have ideas that we are in control, so we stress, and we worry, and we face our past and we relive, or we look to the future with anxiety thinking we can control anything. We do it out of safety. But no one set point is fully determined through your ego and your mind.

So, while we'll do our best to try and make things happen and force things to happen, we forget that it's our higher mind that sees all. If we were to relax just a little bit more, we would be guided to higher timelines where things are more effortless, more joyful, more meaningful, easier. But that requires pushing your mind to the side and relaxing in the presence of what is.

N: Yes. So, it's a powerful lesson not just for right now, but she can take it with her many moments to come.

I'd like to talk more about A's adrenal fatigue. What has been causing this?

A: Stress to be somewhere she's not meant to be yet. Forcing things to happen that are not meant to happen yet. Controlling things that cannot be controlled. Narratives that feel like static in the frequency of what she wants. And trying to control that story out of fear of what people will think of her, out of fear of scarcity. And then remembering that none of it really matters because we came here to exist, to be, and to relax into the present moment in a world that's been conditioned to move as quickly as possible. If you control nothing, what could you create?

N: Now that she knows the meaning of her adrenal fatigue, can we heal and release this for her now? (Yes.)
Go ahead and do that and let us know how you're doing that as you do it.

A: I'm rewiring certain neural pathways, rerouting certain thoughts, tying together new ideas and beliefs that have never been connected. Adding in a command of rest, tasking her brain with ways to seek out more restfulness... to search for peace and harmony over chaos and control. I'm embedding commands for deep rest and sleep to rejuvenate every cell in the deepest restfulness sleep.

N: Is A noticing anything as you do this?

A: It feels kind of heavy and peaceful. Kind of like what I think it would be like floating in the Dead Sea where you're on top of the water, and the sun is hitting your body, and you feel the rays, and it's so warm and kind of glittery.

N: What will she notice or feel after today's session?

A: More patience, deeper breaths. It's like when things happen, she will be more flexible in her state. She won't be as reactive emotionally because the embedded command of it doesn't really matter… will flow through.

N: And no more adrenal fatigue?

A: If she wishes to release it by prioritizing rest and recovery.

N: Yes, but we can release it for her now, right? It's just whether she wants it to come back or not.

A: Yes. The path of least resistance. Take the path of least resistance.

N: Yes. There's no rush. Is this now healed?

A: [She needs to be] taking thoughts from her head and blowing them away. There is a piece of her, a part of her, that holds onto exhaustion because she makes it mean something about her story.

She makes it mean exhaustion is productive when it is the opposite. And untethering those cords in that way, so she sees that it's not a truth, but a corruption of the energy and the energetic pathways. It is not in our nature to be exhausted. Releasing corrupted thoughts.

N: Go ahead and continue doing that, and I'd like to also ask about A's knee. What has been causing her knee pain?

A: The pressure to perform at all costs. The pressure to be at everyone's beck and call. But you can only be supported for so long internally until what carries the brunt of your weight can no longer hold you. But who will hold you if you've held everyone else?

It is okay to ask and seek help because you're not meant to carry the weight of the world, as no single soul is. It's the reminder to not have knee-jerk reactions and to instead take a step back and relax.

N: So, it's more than just the sports?

A: It manifests on the physical plane because some people need that to take you to such an extreme in order to recalibrate and choose a different path. Because if it's physical, it feels real, versus if it's energetic and ethereal. Some people need to be taken to pain in order to choose something different.

N: Yes. Otherwise, we'd say, "I'll get to that later." And some people still do with the pain... but A doesn't need to experience that pain, does she?

A: No. But that would require healing the emotional turmoil she holds with her father.

N: And how can she do that?

A: She needs to forgive him truly, deeply from the seat and center of her soul in the depth of her heart, knowing that he is but a child in an adult body who elected to teach her certain lessons from the most loving, compassionate places of his soul to help her grow to be who she was meant to be on the planet. That he would be so generous in delivering such density, not knowing as a human but as a soul what it would do for her.

N: Yes. That's not easy for him to have to play that role, is it?

A: No. But how would she be so loving if she didn't experience the opposite? How would she be so compassionate and hold space for people who have caused enormous pain to other people if they couldn't look for forgiveness or to be helped by someone who has been abused?

How could people who have been abused feel safe with someone who's never experienced such density? It's her willingness to speak to those wounds and those pains so that everyone can feel a sense of connection, a sense of peace in the pain.

N: So, once A can fully forgive her father, it will heal her knee? (Yes.)

Can we give her some healing today around this to get her started? (Yes.)

Go ahead and do that and let us know what you're doing as you do that.

A: I'm pulling out thorns from her knee. There are thorns of past pain she's unwilling to let go of. So, she placed them there to remember that when the pain hits, that there's something to be healed, but it's internal.

A lot of these wounds are from carrying the brunt and the weight of her family, but she did her best and [needs] to trust that they are supported in their own ways as well, and to not be the sole person carrying them.

So, I'm pulling those thorns out because it feels like thorns from experiences that she did not know were part of what would make up a rose in its beauty, because she was only focused on the pain. And [I'm] putting golden light in the center of the knee with codes from the temple.

N: And is A feeling or sensing anything as you do this?

A: They're warm, and it feels just like tingles. There's a lightness to the energy, and my muscle just spasmed, and that felt like, "Yes. Right."

N: What will she notice after today's session when it comes to her knee pain?

A: She won't necessarily notice the knee. She'll notice the levity in her heart... towards, specifically, her father.

N: Is there anything she needs to say to him to complete the process, or is this more of an internal understanding with herself?

A: She needs to connect to his soul to connect to the higher parts of him. Not necessarily forgiving him in person because he won't necessarily understand, but it's the higher heart within him that knows - and to communicate telepathically and from a heart-centered place total and complete love and forgiveness and understanding and awareness of the experiences they both were gifted.

N: Yes, because [how negatively he treated her] was meant to be a gift even though it didn't appear that way... it didn't feel that way.

A: Not all gifts are wrapped in gold. Some are wrapped in paper. Some are gifted in bags. It is in our ability to receive the gift and not in our judgment of what it does or does not look like that will change a lot for so many. You can also be given gifts wrapped in gold and lace, but the gift inside may not be something that you've wanted or ever thought you needed, but that does not make it a gift any less.

N: A has also noticed that her right ear is a lot more sensitive and has given her the ability to hear beyond the physical world. Is there anything you'd like her to know about that?

A: We are tuning to the frequencies of light and helping her become more aware of the frequencies, and how they feel will help her belief structures to realize she is always receiving information from Spirit.
But she needed the physical reminder of feeling that pressure to feel what it feels like to receive information in that way, so that, in the future, she will trust it completely without needing the physical reassurance of

the certainty of what she is receiving. It is like training wheels.

N: So, there's nothing physically wrong with her?

A: No. It is a fine-tuning, a refining of the information so that she can develop the trust. That is all.

N: Amazing. Can we go ahead and do a final body scan of the whole body, moving from the top of the head to the bottom of the feet, doing a scan and letting us know if there's anything else we need to be concerned about, any problems, or anything that might be out of balance?

A: I'm seeing the pituitary gland light up. It's something to be aware of. More people's pituitary glands are coming online. It's just the inner knowing that consciousness is rising and part of that gland is to help us see, hear, feel beyond the veil.

N: So, is she experiencing any pain in that area?

A: No, it is just the knowing. That is also for you.

N: Okay. So, it's stronger. Anything else you're noticing in the body?

A: There is just a sense of peace... and grounded peace... is what it is? Yes. Perfect.

N: Beautiful. Is there anything else you'd like A to know about her body?

A: The more relaxed the body, the more present the mind. It is simple to say, but complex in a busy environment. Prioritizing rest and relaxation brings forward new thoughts, new ideas, new offerings, new ways of being... because it's the relaxed, less reactive state that will move things more quickly.

Because it is paradoxical in nature to want to control and to speed things up and to get to the destination more quickly whereas relaxing and surrendering changes timelines more rapidly because there is no pressure to control. It is only Spirit-led. But how does one hear their spirit if it's always noisy?

N: Yes. Before we go, are there any last messages you'd like to share with A today?

A: Who are you being in a world that is not ready for light? In a world that finds safety in darkness, who are you being? What do you stand for? Even when the world is not ready.

Fire was gifted to the Earth at a certain point in time, and people were fearful of it, and then they grew to love it. If everyone has an ember inside of them that is ready to burn, who are the ones who gift a part of their fire to those who are ready to receive it? And what kind of courage does it take to break the mold to blaze as brightly as possible and to be an absolute wildfire in the world?

There are those who go and step forward first, knowing that those with the embers who are curious and ready will be willing to receive more magic, more oxygen, more fire. And they will ask you to burn even brighter because of what it means for themselves to burn as brightly as well. Not everyone wants light, but that does not mean it should not be seen. That is all.

Chapter 4: The Life Review & Pre-Planning Process

The process of planning our lives before we enter them involves much consideration. Our pre-life planning decisions are based on what we have already learned in the past, what we wish to learn moving forward, and how we can best support the relationships we have formed with others in our soul group as we incarnate into Earth school.

My client, H, was just as curious as I was to understand how this pre-planning process works. In fact, getting more information about what happens as we plan our lives was one of the main questions she brought to the session for her Higher Self to answer, and I was delighted we got to explore it together in such great detail.

H was first shown a past life where she was a healer who used herbs and the power of the sun, in a very unique way, to heal the few remaining survivors in a war-torn village, many of whom were children. In that life, she worked out of an abandoned church, which became her makeshift healing clinic, because most of the other buildings in her town had already been bombed. This is where she administered her homemade tinctures and tonics to heal the wounded.

She was skilled at what she did, and the work was very rewarding in that prior incarnation. However, it was a life marked by immense loss and loneliness due to losing all of her family and friends in the war, and it was one she was eager to move on from. We moved from that life immediately into the afterlife where H began her life review and the process of planning for her next life.

N: What do you do after you leave the body?

H: My soul floats up. It's like I don't even know that body anymore. It's not alive. It floats up and up through the sky first, then the stars. It looks like layers. It's like very distinct layers.

N: Tell me about the layers.

H: It's like the sky and clouds. It's like a straight layer of all these clouds and then there's black space. It's beautiful, though. I feel like I could just stay there.

N: Does anyone come to meet you?

H: I can hear people saying my name above.

N: What do you feel drawn to doing now?

H: Watching the galaxy and slowly going back up because I've been here before. I enjoy looking at this view because I remember it from the other times I've died. I like moving over—transitioning, whatever—going through this part. Yeah, this is my favorite part, like the galaxy.

N: What do you like about it?

H: It's just pretty. It's like a swirl of magenta and purple and pink-purple and the stars, and it's moving a little bit. It's just peaceful.

N: Where do you go after you enjoy the view?

H: Going upward? I think I'm swimming upward and I'm young again.

Oh, it's my main guide, Swami. He said something funny, and I'm laughing. He's laughing, too. I feel like I've been here so many times.

N: What happens next?

H: I'm sitting on a couch. (Laughs) There's a projector, a TV, and we're going to have popcorn. I think we're going to go over it. It's like a life review. I just feel like I've done this so many times with him. It's like my routine.

Weird. My Higher Self is there, too, but I would think *I'd* be my Higher Self, but I guess I'm not my Higher Self in this. It's like him, my Higher Self, and me.

N: As you're looking back at that life, what did you learn from it?

H: (Bursts out crying) That I'll still survive even if I feel very alone... and I'm very protected.

N: Why was it important for you to experience loneliness in that life?

H: In future lives, other lives... they're showing it like a cloak, like a layer to add on. It's like they're showing it in the way of clothes.

N: It's going to help you in future lives?

H: Yeah. We need to know what it feels like.

N: Almost like it adds to your armor in a way? (Yes.)

Besides experiencing loneliness, what do you think was the purpose of that lifetime?

H: To help others. Share my medicine. To feel the flowers... feel things, and smell them and the sun. The sun feels like a friend, like an old friend. We've worked together a lot and I can only feel the sun like that on this [planet]... on Earth. It's a certain feeling.

N: [The sun] feels different in other places?

H: Yeah. It doesn't feel the same... it feels different, but it feels the best on Earth. The sun makes me feel less alone.

N: What did you do when you were working with [the sun] before?

H: Egypt. We reflected the sun off square metal and directed it using the sun's rays.

N: For what purpose?

H: Healing, but also we could hurt people with it, and we could burn people.

N: Why would you need to do that?

H: I was a man. Because someone told me to. I had to, it was like a job. I was good with using this equipment. (Wonders to herself) I don't know if I created it?

N: So then you got a chance to use the power of the sun to heal? (Yes.)
 Is there anything else that stands out as you review that life with your guides?

H: Helping children was important. Yeah, it feels like a theme. I do it a lot. I didn't have my own kids, but they felt like my own kids. I was close with them.

N: Yes. What do you do after you review the life?

H: We're sitting at a long table. It's just me and Swami, and my Higher Self again. We're discussing what to do next. What I want to do next.

N: What are you saying?

H: We're talking about India, one of those lives again. I'm saying I don't want to do that. It feels very relaxed, nonchalant. I can kind of pick what I want to do.

N: Why don't you want to go to India?

H: Boring! (Laughs) I've done many [lifetimes] there.

N: Been there, done that?

H: Yeah. Russia's coming up for some reason. No, I don't want to do Russia... China, no.

N: Is there a theme to the places that are being listed out? Is there a reason for these particular countries to be called out?

H: Yeah, they were past places that I've been to. I've had lives there and I don't want to go back to any of them. I'm thinking about China.

N: What feels like the next stage of your learning that you want to explore? What lessons?

H: Healing, helping. I get the sense I want something easier after that previous one. I feel like I want to kind of coast in the next one. I think that's why we're joking. I want to be a female and a witch. I think I'm doing England.

N: And how does the process of planning this life in England go?

H: There's family at the table. More people join this big table. Yeah, it's like my siblings—my current siblings—and my parents and my ex-partners. There's a lot of people now. It's a very big room.

N: What is the purpose of all these people coming to join?

H: They decide if they want to join this [life]… or what they want to be in this life, if they're coming or not. Some of them… I get the sense they can choose. I joke a lot.

N: So, it's not a serious process?

H: No, it doesn't feel like it. I think, in the beginning, it was very serious. The earlier stages of it were more serious.

N: What made it more serious?

H: I had many lessons to learn. Now, I think I'm more used to it. It's like the coats - all the layers. I have more layers.

N: So, you mean when you used to go through this process for other lives in the past, it was more serious then, but now you're used to it.

H: But I also earned it. I get the sense they're showing layers on this coat. It's not a coat, but it is. It's like each life I'm gaining a new layer of wisdom. I have many.

THE LIFE REVIEW & PRE-PLANNING PROCESS

N: Do you get to choose which layer you want to add next?

H: Yes, but I feel like I have a lot of them. My main guide and I discuss it, but it feels like we're kind of running out of options. I feel like I have done a lot.

N: Is it like the bottom of the barrel, like the ones you didn't want to work on before?

H: No, those I did. This is more to help other people. I feel like I'm the helper. I'm helping other people add more layers to their coats.

Wow, that's cool. Yeah, I kind of get to pick whatever I want to do because I'm a helper, and I don't get the sense that everybody is like that, so other people are working on their layers, too. Because I've worked on all of mine, it makes it easier to help others earn theirs. So, everyone is picking what layer they want to work on, how we're going to meet, and how I'm going to help them.

N: Can you give an example of one of these exchanges?

H: They're like... dating. One of them, I'm showing him love. He's learning a lot from me. That's one of my favorite layers to help someone get.

N: What are some examples of layers that you've already added? I know there are many.

H: Compassion, trust, loneliness, loyalty. Being a mother is a layer. Being an animal is a layer. Being paralyzed, losing a leg or something is a layer. There are so many different layers.

N: And how do you know that you've earned the layer sufficiently?

Are you judged on having done it or is it more about just having the experience?

H: Both. We don't like that word "judge". No, we discuss it.

We used to not joke or go watch it as a movie with the popcorn. It used to be serious after [the lives], not in a mean way. We would show the people who the lessons were with or how I earned that layer.

The layers, I think, become part of my aura. It's like they're showing me in a material way, but it looks like it becomes part of my aura. So, you can see it, too... energetically.

But yeah. You discuss it together with [your guide]... it seems like I always discuss it with this main guide, Swami.

N: Has he been with you for all of your lifetimes?

H: He's laughing, yes. I think he was my dad. He was my first dad in life. I don't get the sense though that anyone is my "parent" there [in this realm]. I feel like everyone is mature and helps each other, and it's more like helpers, like mentors.

N: Yes. That's what I was going to ask. Why did all of your souls choose to be connected in this group? All these people in this group, around the table, chose to be connected. Are they just connected to you or to each other as well?

H: Both. They choose. We kind of arrange if they want to be in my life. Some of my lifetimes they are, some of them they're not. Some of them... they're in different places... we can interact briefly in passing, but I'll never see them again. Whereas in other lives, they were very close to me. I get the sense that when we exchange, we walk by each other, there's something that happens energetically.

I'm seeing a square, a peg, something that's filling a hole when we pass. Yeah, with our closest best friends and lovers, the pegs are in the heart. It's a bigger thing. Some people are more subtle, smaller pegs, but the heart—the big ones that you meet—they're big. They're more impactful.

N: Yes. So what are you deciding for this next life?

H: England. Wealthy. Wear fancy dresses. One of the men may be like the paperboy or my neighbor or something. My sister's going to be my sister there. My sister currently, she's going to be there with me a lot.

N: Do you pick what time period? (Yes.)
What were your reasons for choosing the particular time period that you are?

H: Easy, light and easy. It is important for me to have a yard, like a nice yard with trees. Nature is very important.

N: You were saying earlier that you felt like you were separate from your Higher Self, that it was like another energy in the room with you. What do you sense is the purpose for that separation?

H: I'm just hearing "ego". My ego. I think to help me understand my earthly, human self. We're the same though. Yeah, we're the same.

N: Would you say it's like you're a layer that's more connected to the Earth?

H: Yeah. She's (the Higher Self) what I've become. I have all the layers, but the layers are her aura. They become her aura.

N: It's almost like you're the Earth representative.

H: Yes, yes. Like 3D. Yes. Like the cloth.

N: What role does the Higher Self have in the planning of the life?

H: It seems more rational... (Thinking for a while)

N: You could ask the Higher Self.

H: What role do you have? "Orchestrate the lessons I need to know for the layers."

N: How is that orchestration done?

H: How is that orchestration done? "It takes many steps, discussion with others, with their souls. Create contracts, discussion with your team, your guides."

N: It's like the networker. (Yeah.)
    Is there anything else you feel called to explore in this state? In this realm?

H: Yeah. There's a land that I like. It's greenery. It's like a field. I enjoy doing that.

N: And this is in the spirit realm?

H: Looks and feels very real, though.

N: What do you do when you're there?

H: I watch the horses. Then there's also a galaxy on the other side that I can watch. It's pretty. I like watching the stars.

N: Is there any other preparation you do before you go into the next life? Do you have to do any studying before you go?

H: I used to. Now I don't feel like I have to do much studying at all. The layers help. The layers are like the studying, but ingrained in us, so it's like you learn and you don't need to study that thing anymore. You can study different parts of it, but once it's ingrained, it's ingrained.

N: And through helping others, do you continue to add more layers to your own aura?

H: Yes, you do. It's not the same, though. They're different kinds of layers. There's many different kinds from what I'm understanding.

N: What makes you choose to want to come back and help as opposed to going off on a different adventure?

H: It's fun, and it feels good when I'm helping. I can't feel like this in this area. Feeling. On Earth, you can feel... like deeply feel. I can feel the benefits of the healing and the help.
Each place feels differently, but this one you can feel it very deeply and I love the sun. Yeah, the sun feels very... the sun was an old friend.

Later in H's session, we discovered that she had come into her current lifetime to help alleviate karma on behalf of her ancestors. Having already learned her own lessons—and earned her own "layers"—did not make her current lifetime any easier because she then decided to take on this earth school learning experience for the purpose of helping others earn theirs.

Chapter 5: Choosing to Embrace Chaos

If we get the opportunity to have a say in the future lifetimes we choose to experience, why would we willingly decide to experience drastic extremes such as wars, destruction, and the illness and death of our loved ones? Why wouldn't we choose to learn our lessons through beauty, bliss, harmony, joy, and love? This is probably because those high vibrational energies, such as joy and love, are already widely present in the spirit realm.

Being on Earth offers a very physical experience where we get to "play" with the full spectrum of emotions. Consider how some people love to watch horror movies for the thrill of the adrenaline rush, even though that is probably not the world they would ideally like to live in. Unless, of course, there is a good reason for making the choice to live in a nightmare-like existence.

J was a unique client living in Israel during the breakout of the Israel-Hamas War, where thousands of soldiers and civilians, including innocent mothers, fathers, and children, have been killed and wounded by bombs nearly every day. She was also dealing with an illness in her family, with her mother slipping further away every day due to dementia. As you can imagine, J greatly struggled with both of these aspects of her life and wondered why she even decided to come to Earth to be surrounded by these horrible atrocities in the first place.

After her Higher Self brought forth visions of prior incarnations, I was able to ask directly why these especially challenging life circumstances were chosen. Why did J choose to come to Earth, and why did she choose such an intense life for herself? The answers that came through can give us a greater understanding of how we are still able to benefit from the horrible things that are happening in the world on a higher soul level, even if they seem unnecessarily harsh or meaningless to our human selves.

N: Why did J choose to live in a place that is breaking out in war?

J: So she can embrace the fact that she is highly sensitive more, and she can feel it to extremes, as she wished for herself. She doesn't remember that. That she can bring her light to the people that need it. That she can spread the love. She's a very loving person, a very caring person. She needs to experience those extremes in order to be sure about how she needs to continue her life and how fragile it is and how important it is for her to continue on her path and do the things that bring her joy.

It's another test for her. She has chosen it and she knows it because she asked this question herself every day since the war started. So, she knows she put herself here for a reason. She kind of figured it out already.

N: Why did she choose to come to Earth in general?

J: She decided to come to Earth to continue expanding, to continue experiencing and feeling things, exploring the human concept. She wanted to bring light to the world, and she believes she has an important mission to do, but she got... she got overloaded. And she doesn't remember all the things that she wanted to do when she is on Earth.

She needs to bring joy to others. She wants to give joy to others and liberation and awakening to people that feel the same as she's feeling here on Earth... to help others find their center by finding herself there first.

She decided to come to Earth because she really wanted to. She wanted to experience it. She is a very brave soul. She knows it's a privilege to be here, but sometimes it's hard for her to comprehend. She will be just fine.

N: It's actually been kind of good research for her to be in these big feelings because she knows what it feels like for other people who are overwhelmed by it as well. She'll be able to help them better, won't she?

J: Exactly. Because she can experience this to such a depth, she can connect to people and give them lots of love and understanding. Something that not everyone can do. But she's a natural at this because of her efforts, which is more appreciated and loved by others than she realizes.

N: Yes. Was it a hard decision for her to come to Earth or was she really excited about it?

J: Not hard at all, but again, when you are in this realm before you incarnate, you don't fully know what is there waiting for you. You know, but you don't know. So, it makes perfect sense for her and for many other beings in the world that they feel that they haven't chosen it, but they really did. It's just sometimes a bit harder than they expect it to be and different.

N: Yeah, you can plan all you want, but what actually ends up happening might not be what you expected?

J: Yes, the human experience is very... it can be very mischievous to be honest.

N: Why don't things always go the way we initially planned before we come to Earth?

J: This is also part of the plan, but the plan that we have goes out and then we need to come up with a different plan even though it's still the same feeling.

It's very complicated to understand it from this perspective, but it's like this difference between having free will and at the same time having a destiny. We all have a destiny, but also we all have free will.

So, when we come here, we just gather in between both of them all the time. So, it feels like no matter what we do, we end up in the same place and at the same time. We end up in the same place by doing different things.

N: I would like to talk about J's mother and her transition. How can J prepare for her mom's transition?

J: She knows that death is not the end. She knows that her mother will always be in her heart and in her dreams and that it's not the end. So, this is not what worries her. What worries her are the emotions, the grief and the sadness… that this is going to overwhelm her because she's already been experiencing them even though her mom is still here. So, the only thing she can do is to cherish the moments that she has with her mom now, no matter how simple they are, even if it's being silent. And to know and to remember that death is not the end. That death is not the end.

She will see her mom all the way in her dreams or her visions during her practices and she'll always be there. So, physically, from a physical point of view, there's not much to do. There will be an impact, a very heavy one, but she's protected by her angels, so she will be okay. She has support, she'll be okay, but she needs to just feel everything that she's feeling now. So when the moment comes, it'll be a bit easier.

N: So, she can prepare through feeling it?

J: Yes, because she's been grieving her mom already for a while, and it's a process. And she knows she's in it, but she needs to continue with this process and she needs to continue to release everything.

N: Why did her mom choose to have dementia?

J: She chose to have dementia because she really wasn't happy with her life. She didn't do things she loved. She conformed to societal expectations and she didn't manage fully to really embrace her own spirit and her own destiny. And it got to the point where she decided that it's no longer acceptable for her to live like that, so she chose to forget and just not be doing it, and she chose not to be so involved like she always was a thousand percent in everything.

That's why she chose this for herself and for others as a reminder of the fragility of life and how important it is to love others because you never know whether they'll depart. And how important it is to really live the life that we came here to live. So, we don't need to forget before our parents depart, hopefully.

N: How can J help her father [through this time]?

J: She's already doing a great job. She can keep sending him prayers. Yes, she can pray for this... for her father.

N: Yes, prayers are very powerful, aren't they?

J: Yes, very much. And she knows that she has not really been doing that because she's been traumatized by the prayers of the Catholic church, so she is having a love/hate relationship with praying.

N: So, this can be a good reminder to her to pray?

J: Yes. And she'll feel much, much better when she does.

N: Thank you for answering my questions. Can we go ahead and do a body scan for J now? Looking through all the areas of the body and just letting us know if there's anything we need to be concerned about. Take your time and do a scan from the top of the head to the bottom of the feet and let us know if there are any problems or anything that might be out of balance.

J: She needs to eat better. She's not eating properly. She needs to eat better because her body is not getting enough nourishment from the food she's eating. So, she needs to eat better because in the long run, there's not a problem now, but in the long run there will be a problem.

N: What would be the best things for her to eat?

J: She eats plant-based. She needs to implement more proteins in her diet. It's something that she knows, but she's kind of sweeping it under the carpet. But I'm saying it now. It's very important to have more proteins in the diet.

N: What's a good example of a protein that would be really good for her?

J: All sorts of beans. Beans and lentils.

N: Are there any other issues that you're seeing in the body?

J: No. She should just check her eyes again because her sight is getting worse. It's her glasses.

N: Why is her eyesight getting worse? What's causing this?

J: She came [in] with perfect vision already. Everyone in her family is having the same issue. It's about not being able to see everything clearly.

N: What is she not seeing clearly?

J: Herself! What she truly is. What a beautiful being she is.

N: Is that the same for her other family members - that they're not seeing themselves clearly?

J: Yes. All of them are connected in this way.

N: Is there anything that she can do to see herself more clearly? To honor what a beautiful being she is?

J: Every time she connects to her heart, she sees what she expects to see. So, every time she can connect to her heart, [through] any practice she chooses that makes her feel connected to her heart, it's going to make her vision clearer.

N: Now that she understands the reason for her eyesight getting worse, can we give her some healing around her eyes now? (Yes.)
    Go ahead and do that and let us know how you're healing it as you're healing.

J: Sending light, yellow light, bright light, even darkness behind closed eyes, strengthening the cells, the blood vessels in the eyes.

N: Is J feeling or sensing anything as you heal this? (Yes.)
    What is she feeling?

J: She can see a lot of colors.

N: The colors? What will she notice after the session?

J: It might take some time, but she should notice improvements. She should notice that her vision… it's a bit less blurry. It can take some time, though.

N: So, whenever she notices she's having trouble with her eyes, does that mean she needs to love herself more? (Yes.)
What are some ways she could show herself that she loves herself?

J: Every time she's choosing something that she genuinely wants and she knows will support her, she's loving herself. Every time she's choosing something that, inside, she knows it's not good for her and yet she's doing it, she is not loving herself.

N: That makes sense. Are there any last messages you'd like to share with J before we go?

J: I really hope that she won't be doubting this experience, that she will truly listen to everything that was said and done today, that it'll encourage her to continue on her journey. She will know that she can always connect to her Higher Self and that she is doing a great job, and she doesn't need to be so harsh to herself for just making mistakes and being human. And that she's very loved. Very much loved.

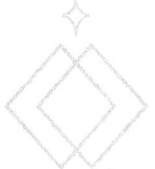

Chapter 6: Healing from Past Incarnations

Although terrible experiences such as war, illness, and death can have a positive effect on our soul growth (even as they traumatize our human selves), there are still times when the wickedness and ignorance of the world have seemingly not benefited us and continue to hinder us. We may even carry the grief from these experiences for multiple lifetimes until we can find the strength to forgive and heal what happened in the past.

This was the case for C, a healer with a fear of being shunned or exiled from society for practicing the spiritual work she did to earn a living. Being exiled due to her healing abilities *had* occurred before in a past life, and her soul remembered it deep down. This fear of exile kept her from sharing more confidently about her intuitive gifts and how she could help others. She subconsciously worried that sharing more about herself would put her life in danger just as it had in past incarnations.

Many ignorant people over the course of human history have so greatly feared the magical abilities that others were exhibiting that they have made an enormous attempt to snuff them out. It's estimated that over nine million people have been burned at the stake for being called witches, including both men and women who exhibited some form of intuitive ability. This usually involved knowledge of how to heal with herbs, a naturally occurring substance given to us in nature.

It is so common for clients to see past lives of being burned at the stake that, as hypnosis practitioners, we were explicitly taught how to hold space for these experiences in our training. No matter how hard society may try to eliminate our inherent intuitive capabilities, they will always come back in another form. Back then, they were called witches. Today, they are called healers.

The fear of openly sharing magical healing gifts with the world continues to hold back our entire collective. This so-called "witch wound" creates an environment that inhibits our intuitive growth because many of the people who are secretly harnessing these abilities are too afraid to share them with others. When we keep quiet about who we are, it makes it more difficult for society to recognize, accept, and normalize the very real possibility that we all have the ability to develop supernatural healing powers. And perhaps, it is not as difficult, unnatural, or "evil" as some people may think. Perhaps the world would be better if we could all tap into our intuition more freely and easily.

Many things that hold us back in our current lifetime are due to experiences from previous times when the world was not as friendly to our type of abilities. We are subconsciously afraid that we are too "weird" or "different" because it was once unacceptable (and even dangerous) to be our true selves. Revisiting these difficult experiences so that we can master ourselves is how we grow. It's also how we help the world evolve, even if it may take a series of lifetimes and hundreds of years of people standing up against the status quo.

We must realize that these life experiences of being exiled, shunned, or even killed for being our authentic selves are still pre-planned precisely because they have something to teach us. The beautiful thing about connecting with the Higher Self through hypnosis is that we can not only discover the root cause of our fears but also create a healing bridge for the Higher Self to help clear away the pain that has resulted from the traumatic experiences that have shaped us in previous lives, as you will see in C's session now.

N: I want you to tell me the very first thing that you see below you or the very first impressions that you have as you come back down to the surface.

C: Big mountains. Lots of green grass. Wide open space. The mountains look familiar—white caps on the mountain.

N: What else is around you?

C: I feel like I don't want to turn around, but I don't know why. When I look in front of me, green grass, mountains. I'm going to try and turn around now.
  [I see] a village down in a valley. I'm on top of a hill, and this is my safe space.

N: If you look down at your feet, what do you see?

C: Brown shoes. Not nice.

N: What are you wearing on your body?

C: A dress—dark green dress—pulled tight at my waist. I wear a gold bracelet on my right wrist and a necklace. A white hat.

N: Are you carrying anything?

C: A basket with flowers gathered from the fields.

N: Does your body feel male or female? (Female)
   Young or old? (Twenties)
   And how does this body feel? Does it feel healthy?

C: Yes. Feels light and strong. My hair's blonde. My skin is bare. I have freckles.

N: What do you feel you're meant to be doing in this place?

C: Healing. People come to see me for my herbs. I know how to find things that other people can't.

N: And that's what you're collecting the flowers for?

C: Yeah. I make elixirs and tonics.

N: What kinds of flowers?

C: Daffodils. Fruits and berries. Things I dig up from underneath the ground with my hands.

N: Are you alone up here? (Yes.)
    Do you live in the village down the hill?

C: No. Not safe for me there.

N: Where do you live?

C: Away. I come to look at the village sometimes from the hill. I come to watch.

N: Do you help anyone in the village? People from there?

C: No. They don't understand what I do. They shunned me.

N: Was there a time that you have been in that village?

C: Yes, I was born there.

N: But now you've left?

C: Yes. They don't understand my gifts. I see things. I see ailments and injuries in people. I see disease. They think that I curse people, but I don't.

N: You're only trying to help. (Yeah.)
   Let's go to the place where you do live, and look at the outside of it, and describe it to me.

C: A brown hut made of wood. I have a fire outside and make things… I make talismans and amulets.

N: Do you live with anyone here?

C: No. I've chosen to be alone. It's safer. Sometimes people come to see me from far away. There are some people who accept me, but they must travel far.

N: Let's go inside your home and describe the interior.

C: Simple table and chairs. The bed in the corner of the room. One room. I have a fire in the center of the room with a cauldron.

N: What do you use the cauldron for?

C: Cooking. I like to cook and make soups, herbal remedies. I can see herbs hanging from the ceiling.

N: What do you do with the majority of your time in this place?

C: I sit and think. I think about people. I think about laws, the laws humans make. I think about my time with people and I enjoy my time without them. They're too complicated for me. I prefer the simplicity of nature and animals. It's easy for me to see patterns in nature. [It] feels predictable and calm to me. People seem unruly and without compassion.

N: Let's go back to the time when you were leaving the village. Be there now and describe to me what's happening.

C: I'm being pushed physically. There are men pushing me on my back, pushing me out. They're calling me a witch.

N: How did they find out that you have these healing abilities?

C: Because I healed someone's eye that had a cataract, and it went from cloudy to clear. And they said that only a witch could do that. It's not natural.

N: Let's go ahead and leave that scene, and let's move forward to an important day, a day that you consider to be important. We've now moved forward to an important day. What's happening?

C: My wedding. I'm getting married to a man who's calm. He understands me. He does not fear me or what I do. I feel safe here.

N: Tell me about him.

C: He's older than me. We have no romantic relationship, but he has chosen to protect me. He recognizes my gifts and sees them as valuable. He does not think that I'm of the devil. He thinks that I'm made by God. He lets me do my work and tend to my garden. He brings people to me.

N: How did you meet this man?

C: I was out walking. We began to talk.

N: As you look into this man's eyes, do you recognize him as someone you know in this life?

C: [Says name of current partner]

N: Beautiful, and tell me how you spend your days together.

C: We walk in the forest. We walk up the hills and mountains. We have a dog. We spend most of our time in nature. I feel lucky.

N: Amazing. Yes. Very lucky. Let's go ahead and leave that scene. Let's move forward to another important day, a day that you consider to be important. Be there now. What's happening?

C: I have a child, a boy.

N: A boy. What are you doing with him?

C: Watching him, watching him play.

N: About how old is he?

C: Three.

N: You had him with your husband?

C: Yes. Our relationship changed over time.

N: It changed and became more romantic... is that what you mean?

C: I let him in. I felt safe with him.

N: Beautiful. Is there anything else happening in this place?

C: Peace. We seclude ourselves from others because it's not safe. We keep to ourselves.

N: It's a peaceful life now. Amazing. Once again, let's leave that scene and move forward to an important day. We've now moved forward to another important day. What's happening?

C: I'm on trial.

N: Tell me more.

C: I'm in a courtroom. I'm in a hole. They're penalizing me for my gifts.

N: They found out about where you were? (Yes.)
    Is it the people from the village?

C: Yes. Someone betrayed me.

N: What happened?

C: They were giving rewards for implicating others in crimes against God. They say that I'm the spawn of the devil and that my gifts are not natural. That I'm not natural. They took me away from my husband and my child. No one can save me now.

N: They were afraid of you?

C: Yes. I do no harm to anybody. I'm very gentle.

N: They're wrong about you?

C: Yes. They put me in prison on the same day.

N: Who is the person who turned you in?

C: It was my friend. She's jealous of me. She has been since we were children. She believes that God will save her. God knows. God knows what you've done.

N: Is this someone that you trusted?

C: She drowned her baby. She's worried that I will tell.

N: Hmm... so she's protecting her own reputation? (Yes.)
   Let's move forward to the last day of your life in this lifetime we are watching. What's happening? What do you see?

C: I'm in the middle of the village standing on the wooden platform. Under the platform, they're putting wood and pieces of dried kindling. I'm praying that I won't feel the pain.

N: Whatever happens next, you can watch it completely as an observer. You will not have any physical sensations. You can talk about it calmly and objectively. What happens next?

C: There's a man who's announcing my sentence. He's yelling. There's a big crowd. They've all come to watch me burn.
   It's a celebrated day. They believe they're overcoming evil. They believe they're performing God's will, that they are soldiers of God.

There's a man entering with a stick that is on fire, wrapped in material at the top of the stick. The crowd is cheering. They're lighting the pyre now. They see my soul leaving my body. I know that I am safe.

N: Yes. What do you do after you leave your body?

C: I go home [as a spirit], I go to see my child and my husband. (Crying) They're being driven out of town.

N: Where are they going to go?

C: Into the hills. There's a village that can keep them safe. There's more people like me there.

N: Did you know about that village when you were living? (Yes.)
   But you felt more safe to be on your own? (Yes.)
   Is there anywhere you have to go now so you know what to do next?

C: I'll be taken home. I can see angels.

N: Are they saying anything to you?

C: They're just smiling.

N: And how do you feel?

C: I regret that those around me did not see me for who I truly was, but I understand.

N: As you look at that life, what did you learn from it?

C: People will penalize what they don't understand. That they will cordon off those that are gifted. There is a great misunderstanding of the other worlds. Many people are dying because they're not receiving the help that's available to them.

N: What do you think was the purpose of that lifetime?

C: Helped me meet my husband and child.

N: There was still some happiness. (Yes.)
    Anything else?

C: I must continue on with my work regardless of any pain that I will endure.

N: Yes, it's only temporary. (Yes.)
    And why must you continue?

C: I have important work to do.

N: What kind of important work?

C: Earth is fraught with pain and suffering. I've come here to help. I have gifts from other places and times that could contribute in the now.

N: Yes. And was it a desire of your soul to be able to contribute those things? Did you choose to bring those gifts here? (Yes.)
    Why did you want to help Earth?

C: Because there is peace and calm "here". I do not know peace and calm "there". I want to help teach this.

N: Yes. So, you have an important mission.

C: Not more important than others. We're all here to help.

N: Yes. And chose to help. (Yes.)

Amazing. Let's move away from that scene now. Leaving the person there to continue on their own path. You can move either forward or backward to find another appropriate time and place (or lifetime) that has information that you need. You're now at another time and place. Where are you now?

C: I'm inside a temple. I'm in Egypt.

N: What do you see as you look around you?

C: I see the place where I work. There are others who do what I do.

N: Tell me about them.

C: We wrap the dead and help them to pass into the other world. It's a very sacred role. I feel at home here because it's quiet.

N: Tell me how you do that.

C: We're given the bodies. We practice ceremony and rituals. We help to preserve the body so that it can live to run again in the other life. I find these practices magical. I'm only learning.

N: How did you come to take on this role?

C: I was chosen. They know that I see the other worlds. I'm here with Imhotep. He's my teacher.

Note: Imhotep was an Egyptian chancellor for the king in the third dynasty and a high priest of the sun god Ra. Known for being a sage, astrologer, and architect who helped develop the pyramids, he became famous for his contributions to medicine after he passed around 2600 BCE.

N: Let's move forward to an important day in this life that you are seeing, a day that you consider to be important. What's happening?

C: I'm helping to preserve a king. This is my first time as an assistant.

N: It's a big honor!

C: Yes. Normally, I stand and observe, but today I am helping to dress his body.

N: How do you feel?

C: Honored. Grateful.

N: Yes. How does your teacher feel and the people around you there?

C: I've been studying under him for many years now. I'm ready to start doing this practice on my own. He'll still watch and guide me, but I'm ready and I've moved through all of the ritual practices and ceremonies to be qualified to step into this position in our society.

N: Beautiful. What is it about your intuitive abilities that make you so good at this role?

C: I can see diseases in the body. I know how to hide them and cover them up to preserve the reputation of the king.

N: How did this king die?

C: Kidney. I see it turning blue.

N: Are you able to know why the kidney problem was caused?

C: He was ingesting poison. He liked to drink.

N: On purpose then?

C: Yes. No. (Thinking)
In our society there is a great desire for pleasure and excess. I do not know how to say this politely. He enjoyed the fruits of his labor, perhaps too much, but we do not judge him for this. This is his right as ruler.

N: Did he have any other health issues that you're able to pick up on?

C: His ankles are deformed. This is all.

N: Okay. What happens with his body after you finish your work?

C: He's wrapped. We embed jewels and symbols in the wrapping. He's then taken to a different place to be put in his tomb.

N: And how do you feel after completing the work?

C: I love my work.

N: Yes. Let's leave that scene and let's move forward to an important day. We've now moved forward to an important day. What do you see?

C: I'm becoming a priest.

N: Are you male or female?

C: Female.

N: And what's happening?

C: My work with Imhotep has continued. I know the ways of the dead. Now, I'll learn how to work with the living. I will step into a role as a priest to help those who live.

N: And how will you do this?

C: I will provide guidance and healing. I will give them wise counsel. I will also perform rituals of magic. I enjoy this role.

N: Yes. And you're honored for it. (Yes.)
   Beautiful. Let's go ahead and move forward to the last day of your life in this lifetime we are watching. What's happening? What do you see?

C: I'm very old now. It has been a good life. My body is ready to expire. (Voice cracks)

N: You can sense it coming? (Yes.)
   What happens next?

C: I pass away in my sleep.

N: And what do you do after you pass?

C: I meet with the Old Ones. We speak about my time. They weigh my heart and it is light. I'm allowed to proceed.

N: And where do you go from there?

C: Into a field of reeds, a place where there's a river. Imhotep is there. He's like my father. I spend my days by the river. I learn.

N: As a spirit?

C: It's another world.

N: What kinds of things are you learning there?

C: Anything that I choose to… from a collection of scrolls.

N: Amazing. Every life has a lesson and from this position you can look back at that entire lifetime, before leaving the body, and see it from a different perspective. As you look back at that life, what did you learn from it?

C: That life can be harmonious.

N: Your gifts were honored there… (Yes.)
   What else made it harmonious?

C: The relationships I had with those around me. There was no one who condemned me for my gifts, no traitors, no one there to sabotage or hurt me. I was in the right place.

N: Yes. Your gifts could really flourish there. You were made to do that job. (Yes.)
   What do you think was the purpose of that lifetime?

C: It showed me the benefits of my skills, allowed me to find my place, to give me a great and wise teacher.

HEALING FROM PAST INCARNATIONS

N: Yes. Anything else?

C: This is enough.

N: I know the Higher Self could have brought forth many different lifetimes for C to see today. You chose to bring forward the herbalist for her to see. Why did you pick that lifetime to show her?

C: This plant medicine is important to her. It's important to her future journey. That life contains information she needs now.

N: What kind of information?

C: About plants, ways to heal current ailments and illnesses that are unrecognized by modern medicine.

N: Yes. So, physical healing is meant to be part of her path? (Yes.) What else were you trying to tell her about her life now?

C: That she can let go of past grievances of those who have hurt and harmed her. These people have repeated across many lifetimes. There was more than one person within that audience that betrayed her. Many of these people are around her now.

N: Is she aware of them?

C: Yes, at subtle levels. It is important for her at this time to remove any weeds from her garden. This is why she feels unsafe because there are many around her at this time who do not wish to see her succeed. It's the same as in that life. This is why I showed her that life.

N: Yes. How will she know who they are?

C: You can feel their betrayal ahead of time. There is a feeling. It's a familiar feeling that she knows. It is wise for her to keep her wits about her. There are many that she can trust, but there are some that struggle with the power they sense within her.

N: Are these people she knows in her physical reality, or online, or both? (Both.)
And how can she weed them out once she feels that they are not good for her?

C: She needs to set energetic and physical boundaries. She needs to very carefully choose, like the herbs she would choose, which ones are good and which are poison.

N: Yes. And how can she set those boundaries?

C: She can uninvite them from her world. She does not need to use words for this. She can simply uninvite them, and then allow the tides to pull them away. It does not need to be violent. It does not even need to be heard or seen.

N: Yes. Is this something that can become very easy for her?

C: Yes. [She] feels she needs to nurture and protect everybody. This is *not* her role.

N: What is her role?

C: To teach.

N: Yes, and then it's up to them what they do with that information. It's not so much a responsibility to heal everyone. (Yes.)

What kinds of things should she teach?

C: The karmic laws, about herbs and medicine, about reincarnation. What she's seen and learned over many lifetimes about personal power protection.

N: So, she's doing a great job because she's doing this, isn't she?

C: Yes, but not confidently yet. She still feels she hasn't found her place. She still doubts the information that comes forward.

N: How can she become more confident?

C: Disregarding other people's perspectives and opinions. Her messages don't need to appeal to everybody. She's not for everybody.

N: Who *is* she for?

C: Those who wish to learn. There are some who feel they already know. These are not her people.

N: You also chose to bring forward the life as the Egyptian priest for her to see. Why did you pick that lifetime to show her?

C: Because this was a lifetime where she felt confident and free, when she had found her place. I wanted to show her that she can find her place.

N: Yes. And how can she do that?

C: She needs to study the herbs. The herbs play a greater part than what she remembers. This is why we've given her the plant medicine, the knowledge of it. It needs to come back. It will not be all that she does, but it will play a significant part.

N: What is so powerful about herbs?

C: They are nature's medicine. They're the way that we will all heal. There is emotional healing and understanding. There is illumination and enlightenment. The plants are teachers and they can help us learn about ourselves and about the world and worlds around us. She's here to help people connect with plants.

N: Beautiful. Is there anything else you were trying to tell her about her life now through showing her the Egyptian priest?

C: She needs to trust that she knows where she's going and what she's doing... to stop looking to others for approval or confirmation. Others will only mislead and misguide her. Only she knows her true path.

N: Why does she look for approval?

C: Because she does not feel safe, and those who do not feel safe seek approval so that they are not consumed by society and law. She needs to realize that she's protected and that she moves outside of society and law.

N: Yes. Much higher laws.

C: Yes. I'm happy we got to meet today.

N: Yes, me too. Where in the world would C's soul be the happiest?

C: There are many places that she would be content, but it is important for her to be amongst nature. She enjoys watching from afar, people in the cities as they move through their lives, but she's much more content in nature. She does not like [her home country] because she has a long history there. It still feels too fresh. It'll be better in older places, older countries, places where Celtic law can be filled.

N: Yes. Will you be guiding her to find her next place? (Yes.)
And she'll know when it's time or can you give her any extra hints?

C: She'll know when it's time. I always give her signals when it's time.

N: So, she can totally trust. (Yes.) She knows she's protected. (Yes.)
What does C need to do to move into complete alignment with her soul?

C: She needs to disregard the outside world wholly and completely. This is not her place to play, and it is not her place to dream. She needs to spend more time in her own inner world with nature, with the plants. This is important. She'll feel less congestion if she moves away from society, and if she cannot move completely away from society, [it is important] that she find ways to do this that are manageable.
N: Yes. Let nature heal her.

C: Yes, we understand she still needs to work and be seen, but it is the unseen worlds, the plant kingdom she needs to connect with, and this can only be done in nature.

N: Yes. How could C shift her work to feel more fulfilled by it, in addition to working with plants and herbs, in terms of a format or a method?

C: This is still to be answered. She has not decided yet. She still believes she needs to gather more information, so she is attracting at this time those trapped in trauma. This is why she wishes to move away from healing. It is taking up too much time and energy. She needs to move in the direction of the pursuit of wisdom, studying and teaching.

N: Yes. Because these healing abilities are available to everyone on some level, right? (Yes.)

And so, through teaching, she can teach a man to fish or just give him fish. Not a good way to say that, but you know what I mean? (Yes.)

So, [teaching] would free up her energy more, is that what you're saying? (Yes.)

How can she let go of the responsibility that she might be carrying to continue with the healings [that she is currently doing for work]?

C: This will not be easy for her as she has juggled this challenge over many lifetimes. She needs to remember that everyone is on their own individual soul's path and that the hardest lessons are part of what others have chosen to come here to learn. It is not her role to take those lessons away. There are some people who are here to learn and some that are here to endure pain and trauma so that they will learn.

N: Are there any other past life gifts that C has had, that would help her most now, that could be reactivated?

C: She has everything she needs. She does not need any more than this. There are gifts and talents she's not yet recognized, but these will come to her over time. She needs to have faith that they'll be delivered in the moment she needs the most.

N: Yes. It's a natural process of reactivation, isn't it? (Yes.)

Beautiful. What about C's interest in archeology? Where does that come from?

C: It comes from her love of history and respect of the past. This is something she could study if she chooses to, but some of the shine and shimmer may come off this if she were to study it in real life. It's still a role that is trapped in society and law, and in human beings' understanding of our mystical and magical past. And as you know, Natalie, human beings understand very little of the ancient histories and legacies we hold.

N: Yes. If you find something really cool, there's always going to be someone who fears it. (Yes.) Or denies it even.

C: Yes. There are many lies.

N: Which is boring! (Yes.) So, archeology is not the best path for her in this lifetime. (No.)
   Let's go ahead and talk about some of C's health issues. What can you say about the skin rashes that she experiences? What's causing this?

C: This is anger unresolved. This is being worked out slowly over time.

N: Where does this originate from? This life or another life?

C: Many lives.

N: When was the very first time the soul experienced this?

C: It reflects through all of her lifetimes apart from a few. There is a fire within her that she needs to learn how to tame and work with.

N: And how can she learn to work with it?

C: She needs to not fear it. She fears that it drives people away. It can draw people closer to her if she uses it as power and not prejudice. She has an aversion to those who seem weak. This is a self-protection mechanism. This will dissolve over time.

N: Is there any significance to when she notices a flare up of the skin rash?

C: When she feels out of control.

N: So is it an important indicator for her to notice when it flares up? (Yes.)
And what is she meant to do in those situations?

C: Needs to ground and meditate and find work that makes her feel joyful. It is through studying and teaching that she will satiate the control that she needs.

N: So, is the rash a sign of being out of balance then? (Yes.)
If she changes her actions, will that then alleviate and remove this issue?

C: Yes. She needs to surrender to her environment and stop trying to separate herself from others.

N: Except the ones who don't have her best interests, right? (Yes.)
But when she doesn't pick up that feeling of betrayal from them, does that mean that they're safe then? How will she know if they're safe?

C: She needs to stop choosing friends full of fire. She needs those who balance her fire. She's still learning how and when to feel safe. There will still be some more burns in the future, but over time she will grow to recognize those who are exhibiting the wrong characteristics, those who are jealous of what she has.

N: Yes. It's a process of learning. It's not the worst thing in the world, it's just something to learn from. (Yes.)

What about the asthma that C has had to deal with throughout her life? What's causing that?

C: Allergies to the world around her. There are also some past life drownings that need to be released.

N: Can we release those now? (Yes.)
Tell me how you're doing that.

C: I'm releasing the memories she stores in her body.

N: She won't have to deal with asthma anymore going forward? (No.)
Thank you. What about the constant food poisoning that C recently had to endure over and over again? What was the purpose of that?

C: She has very sensitive gut health. This needs to be monitored. Fruit and vegetables are not completely safe. There are poisons applied to them. It would be ideal for her to seek out medicine through food that has not been touched by human hands or that has very minimally been touched by human hands. Anything that is mass produced is no longer safe and clean.

N: Is there anything else she can do to improve her gut health on the occasion where the purest food isn't always available?

C: Leafy green vegetables will help to rebuild what she has lost.

N: How often?

C: Every day.

N: And how long will it take for her to notice a change?

C: Three months.

N: Thank you. What about how C has constantly been feeling so tired and not sleeping well? What is causing this?

C: Because she works in her sleep. She ventures into other places and lands.

N: Is there a way she can do that that would be less draining on the body in *this* land?

C: Ask her guides to allow her to sleep at night. She needs at least three to four nights every week of sleep where she's not traveling to other places and times. This is something she can ask her guides for help with.

N: Yes. She can still get plenty of work done on the other nights. (Yes.)
   That is enough, right? (Yes, yes.)
   Thank you. C has also been experiencing some issues with her speech since childhood that has re-emerged for her. What's causing this?
C: She fears that she'll say the wrong thing as saying the wrong thing in the past has driven others away. She feels her tongue is cursed, therefore she would prefer not to speak, not to say anything at all, than to get something wrong. This has been further confirmed in this life through moments of anger where she'd said things she wishes she had not said.

N: Can we give her a clearing for this now? (Yes.)
   Let me know how you're doing that.

C: I'm clearing past memories of times when she has spoken out of turn, where she has said inflammatory things to others even if they were true. I'm clearing memories of others' bad reactions to words that she's said.
   This is what holds her back. She worries what others will do to her

if she speaks. It has made it harder for her to embrace her gifts as her channeling is spoken. This is why she prefers to write so that she can filter everything that is said before it is seen. She does not filter anything in her writing, but it helps her body to feel safe.

N: Yes. Is C feeling or sensing anything as you heal this? (No.)
What will she notice after this session?

C: That speaking will come easier to her. It does not need to be overthought.

N: Will she be able to start a podcast or is that even meant to be part of her path?

C: Not yet. It's not time yet.

N: And C has had her nose broken a number of times. What is the reason for this?

C: There is no reason for this.

N: What's caused it?

C: Her head is just sometimes in the wrong place at the wrong time. This is nothing to be concerned or alarmed about. Just childhood injuries.

N: Okay, thank you. And what about C's heavy periods? What caused that?

C: The releasing of trauma and energy. This will be coming to a close soon. There's nothing for her to worry or be concerned about. Just a physical release of energy. She also passes in her blood, the energy of others. This is why it's so heavy.

N: So there is no longer a reason for that to happen anymore then? (No.)
Will she still need to release other people's energy in other ways? (Yes.)
And how can she do that?

C: Through speaking.

N: So, speaking is healing for her? (Yes.)
Beautiful. Let's go ahead and do a scan of the body, if that's alright? (Yes.)
Looking through all the areas of the body and just let us know if there's anything we need to be concerned about. Do a scan from the top of the head to the bottom of the feet and let us know if there's any problems or anything that might be out of balance.
C: Her kidneys are weak. This can be fixed through plant medicine.

N: What caused that issue?

C: It's genetic from her mother's side.

N: Why did that gene begin or where did it come from?

C: Is connected to grief. Grief that has been passed down from many generations above her.

N: Can we give her some healing for it today? (Yes.)
Tell me what you're doing as you do that.

C: Helping her to release more grief from her body. Disconnecting her from the family tree so that grief is not being passed down, particularly from her mother.

N: Can we go ahead and heal that backwards and forwards on the family line? (Yes.)

Thank you. And then she's to use herbs to continue the healing? (Yes.) And she'll know which ones to use? (Yes.)

Thank you. Are you noticing any other issues in the body?

C: She's otherwise well.

This session was a beautiful reminder that we have had lives of trauma, as well as lives of healing. We've had lives where we were not accepted for who we are, and we've had lives where we were greatly honored for our gifts. When the Higher Self shows both sides, it does so to promote balance and integration between the two within the current lifetime. It reminds us of the healing that is possible.

We had such a strong connection with C's Higher Self in this session that, once all of her main questions were answered, the opportunity was taken to ask about some of the more major questions many of us have about the nature of reincarnation and how the cycle of coming to have lifetimes on Earth officially stops.

N: C and I are both curious. How do we stop reincarnating? What can you tell us about that process? Because I assume we chose to be here for a reason.

C: The process ends when the learning ends. If there is still more to learn, then there are more reincarnations to move through. We come to Earth to see life from different angles, to be in different positions in society and culture, to learn, to observe, to develop compassion, to fully move into the heart, to respect the soul and to move with it. To not allow the body to rule and run the show.

You will both stop reincarnating when you feel that you've learned enough. But for now, both of you are not yet satiated. There are more lifetimes still to learn, to observe, and to teach.

N: Yes, it can be exciting! (Yes.)

Does everyone reincarnating need to learn the same lessons on Earth or do we kind of create our own curriculum?

C: You create your own curriculum. This is done in accordance and attendance with your guides and those who monitor your path. You are not all here to learn the same lessons. You each come with an area of apprenticeship that then becomes mastery.

N: Yes. So, when you say that us being satiated stops the cycle, it's our choice. It's like you're making sure we get to learn what we want to learn. (Yes.)

And our guides assist with that. (Yes.)

We just forget sometimes, don't we?

C: Human beings become frustrated with the path. They forget the curriculum they've chosen and because lessons seem disconnected, they lose focus. This is why it's important to observe the soul as the soul is the being that keeps human beings on their path.

N: Yes. It was mentioned in the past life as the Egyptian priest... this imagery of weighing the heart. Could you explain more about that?

C: This is a process that is unique to particular beings. This process is a metaphysical vision and representation of the deeds enacted in this lifetime. It is an entryway into another school, another school of learning. If the heart is light, then entry is gained. If the heart is heavy, then the soul is moved to a different place to learn.

N: So, it's not the end of reincarnating, it's just graduation into a different area?

C: Yes. A different school.

N: Thank you. Before we go, are there any last messages you'd like to share with C today?

C: You may choose to come and speak to me at any time. I'm always here. Thank you for this opportunity to speak with C today. Thank you for bringing forth your gifts to help those around you.

Chapter 7: Parallel Lives on Other Planets

Every conversation with the Higher Self is an opportunity to learn something new that pushes us beyond our comfort zone and refreshes our concept of what we thought we knew about the world. The witch wound is very common, and as I would eventually come to discover, so are lifetimes on other planets.

While healing with plants is no longer considered to be witchcraft or the work of the devil, the idea that we have had past lives on other planets is still not generally well-accepted. After all, our scientists have not yet discovered other planets that can safely support complex lifeforms. Still, that doesn't mean they don't exist. Lifetimes on other planets have come up multiple times in sessions, often occurring immediately alongside lifetimes based in well-known time periods that we can easily verify as having occurred in our human history on Earth.

My conversation with J and her Higher Self opened up more questions than it answered about the nature of the universe and of ourselves as multidimensional beings living in parallel realities on Earth and elsewhere. As I guided J into her first vision, she didn't see anything at first. I won't lie and say that I wasn't panicking a bit as a fairly new hypnosis practitioner. I continued to ask her to look around and describe what she saw. Eventually, with patience, an image began to materialize in her mind's eye as she allowed herself to slip deeper into trance.

J: I'm just seeing black…

There's stone walls. There's a window. There's bars on it, and there's just some sunlight coming through. I feel dizzy. I can look out the bars and see the ocean. There's a cliff. It's on the side of a cliff.

N: What else do you see out there?

J: The cliff's really sharp. There's rocks at the bottom. There's gulls flying around. There's just ocean for miles. It's lonely.

N: Is there anyone else around you in this place?

J: No. I am the only one in there. I just have rags. I'm wearing rags.

N: As you look down at your feet, what do you see?

J: Stone floor, dirty, no shoes.

N: Does your body feel male or female? (Female.)
    Young or old? (Young woman.)
    How does this body feel? Does it feel healthy?

J: No. Skinny, malnourished.

N: Do you feel you've been in this place for many days?

J: Yes. For some time.

N: Do you ever have any human contact?

J: No, not often. There is a guard, but not often.

N: What do you feel you're meant to be doing in this place?

J: I'm a prisoner.

N: A prisoner? Can you remember back to the reason why you're here?

J: Unacceptable gifts. Collecting herbs.

N: How did they discover this about you? Did other people see you doing these things? (Yes.)
   Were these people who lived near you? (Yes.)
   Were they people that you knew?

J: Yes, people I'd helped.

N: So, they turned you in? (Yes.)
   Had you ever heard of anyone else not being allowed to use these gifts before?

J: No, this was new to me.

N: So, you didn't know you were doing anything wrong? (No.)
   Do you feel like you did anything wrong? (No.)
   What kinds of things were you helping people with?

J: Babies. Ailments. Sickness.

N: How did you learn how to work with herbs in this way?

J: My mom.

N: She taught you? (Yes.)

Does your family know where you are?

J: I'm the only one left.

N: You're the only one left. Do you remember what happened to the rest of your family?

J: There was a great sickness. They died.

N: The sickness... is that something you were trying to help with... with the herbs?

J: Yes, but I couldn't stop it.

N: But you didn't get the illness?

J: Yes, but not as bad.

N: Were you sick when you came into this place?

J: No. That's why I was put there.

N: Because you were able to heal from it? (Yes.)
 Thinking back to where you used to live before you were in this place, go outside of your home or wherever you were residing and look at the outside of it. Can you describe it for me?

J: Yes. It's small. A thatched roof. A hut outside in a forest. Dirt roads. Olden day dress. Chickens, animals, small village.

N: Did your family live there with you?

J: I lived there alone.

N: Alone? Go inside of your home, open the door and describe the interior to me.

J: It's mud. Not brick, but mud walls, small table with a stool, a fire, a bed by the fire, and herbs drying from places around the house. Bundles of them.

N: Did you always live in this home? Did you grow up here?

J: Yes, just my mom and I.

N: Just your mom. And you didn't have any siblings?

J: No. They died.

N: You did, but they died?

J: Small, when they were young.

N: About how old are you when you go into this prison area?

J: Thirties.

N: Do you know who told them about you?

J: Someone whose family member I couldn't help.

N: Were they upset with you? (Yes.)
    Was this a person you had trusted?

J: Someone I'd helped many times.

N: And they turned on you?

J: Yes, a king, his men came. They called me a witch.

N: A witch. Did you say anything back to them?

J: Just that I was helping people.

N: And then what happened?

J: I was dragged out of my home and taken to this place.

N: How are you feeling when this is happening?

J: Confused, scared, unsure.

N: And no one will listen to you. They all think what they're doing is right?

J: No one speaks up. Even if the villagers disagree, they say nothing.

N: Is there some sort of law against healing people?

J: Not a law as such, but there is starting to be more people accused of similar things.

N: But you had never seen this degree of punishment occur before? (No.)
    Let's go ahead and leave that scene, and let's move forward to the last day of your life. Now we've gone forward to the last day of your life in this lifetime we are watching. What is happening?

J: They're getting ready for... to burn me.

N: You don't have to feel any physical sensations. You can watch it completely as an observer if you want to. And tell me what happens next.

J: I'm tied to a stake, and they set the sticks alight below me while people stand around and watch.

N: What are you thinking when this is happening?

J: How did it come to this? How did we get here from medicine that was passed down from generation to generation to this... and betrayal?

N: Betrayal. Yes. Are you angry?

J: Sad.

N: As you look around at the people who are doing this to you, can you see their faces?

J: Some of them, but some are hiding their faces.

N: They don't want to watch?

J: No, it's more that they have a mask on. The people setting the fire are wearing black, they have masks, but the villagers... some are looking on with agreement, others with horror.

N: Can you recognize anyone out there? (No.)

Okay. Let's go ahead and move through to the other side. You've now left your body, and whatever has happened has already happened, and you're on the other side of it. As you look at that life, what did you learn from it?

J: That people fear what they don't understand, and that intention is sometimes not enough to fight fear.

N: What do you think was the purpose of that lifetime?

J: I think the purpose was forgiveness.

N: Forgiveness. Now that you're on the spirit side, do you have forgiveness for the people who did this to you?

J: Yes. Those people were manipulated by other people.

N: Is there anywhere you feel like you're meant to go from here as you leave the body?

J: For a rest.

N: Rest. Okay, let's move away from the scene now. Leaving the person there to continue on their own path, you can move either forward or backward to find another appropriate time and place that has information that you need. You are now at another time and place. Where are you now?

J: England.

N: England? What do you see around you?

J: Hills, greenery, people. Rich people, like courtesan-type people.

N: What are you doing in this place?

PARALLEL LIVES ON OTHER PLANETS

J: I work there.

N: As you look down at your feet, what do you see?

J: Beautiful shoes, red shoes.

N: And what do you see that you're wearing on your body?

J: Beautiful clothes, corset, big skirts, lots of jewelry.

N: Tell me about the jewelry.

J: Pearls. Big stone—purple stone—and rings. My hair is done elaborately.

N: You're a female? (Yes.)
   Do you feel young or old?

J: Young.

N: And does this body feel healthy?

J: Yes. Strong, fit, healthy. Nourished.

N: Nourished, yes. You said that you think you're there for work. What do you do for work?

J: A lady in waiting for [Queen] Elizabeth I.
   We're going for a walk through the gardens. It's a whole group of us. We walk with Elizabeth. She conducts business while we walk behind her.

N: Have you been doing this work for a long time?

J: Since I was a child, a teenager.

N: Do you remember how it came about that you took on this role?

J: My father is important. I was born for that.

N: Okay. Do you like this job? (Yes.)
What do you spend the majority of your time doing?

J: Embroidery. Walking. Sewing.

N: Do you live in the same place as Elizabeth? (Yes.)
Do you have your own room? (Yes.)
Nice. Okay. Let's go ahead and move forward to an important day, A day that you consider to be important in this life. We have now moved forward to an important day. What is happening? What do you see?

J: Elizabeth has died. I'm kneeling by the bed, holding her hand in tears.

N: Had you been close with her?

J: Yes. Friends for many years.

N: Do you know how she died? (No.)
Was it unexpected?

J: She was sick for some time. She was getting worse.

N: About how old would you say she is?

J: Seventy?

N: Older woman? (Yes.)
  What do you do now that you've discovered this?

J: I've been waiting for this for days. She had been sick, but I don't know what I will do now. I don't know another life.

N: Let's move forward and see what you do next.

J: I leave the castle. I'm in another house, a large house, but I'm very unhappy.

N: What do you spend your time doing there now?

J: Sitting by the window looking out.

N: Are you familiar with the people you live with there?

J: Yes. But they're not family.

N: Not family. And they took you in after you left the castle? (Yes.)
  Do you like living in this place?

J: It is comfortable, but I'm not happy.

N: Tell me about that.

J: Elizabeth was my friend, was the life I've only ever known, and I don't know what to do with myself now. My grief is overwhelming. I can't find happiness. She doesn't live much longer. The end was spent in grief.

N: Let's move forward to the last moment in this lifetime we're watching. What's happening? What do you see?

J: There's a four-poster bed. It's very sweaty and hot, and there's some sort of illness.

N: You can go ahead and watch it as an observer without any physical sensations and tell me what happens next.

J: She dies in the bed.

N: Looking down at the body, what does she do now?

J: She's just lying there. People pull the sheets over her head. She's pretty old. Seventies.

N: So, she lived a long life of service.

J: Mostly happy.

N: Mostly happy until the end. As you look at that life, what did you learn from it?

J: Friendship. Loyalty. Love.

N: And what do you think was the purpose of that lifetime?

J: I think the purpose of that lifetime was the supporting of another. My life was in service and support for someone else.

N: Yes. What did you learn from that experience of supporting another person?

J: It was rewarding. It was a happy life. It was privileged in a time of great hardship, and I was grateful for that. So, in my service, I also benefited from that service. It was two-way.

N: Beautiful. Now, let's drift away from that life. Drifting and floating away from that life, leaving the courtesan there to continue on her own journey.

I know the Higher Self could have brought forth many different lifetimes for J to see today. You chose first to bring forward the life of the herbalist who became a prisoner for her to see. Why did you pick that lifetime to show her?

J: Being your authentic self can sometimes draw toward you criticism, punishment. Do them anyway. Follow your path—your calling—regardless of the situation around you. Even when it's not safe to do so.

N: Follow your calling even when it doesn't feel safe. (Yes.)

How does that relate to decisions or choices she's making in her life right now?

J: Going against narratives is always dangerous in that it draws criticism to you from those who never question. If you question, you'll be criticized, but if you go with the narrative, you'll never grow.

N: Yes. So, she's meant to ruffle feathers a little bit with things that she's meant to share? (Yes.)

You also chose to bring forward the life as the courtesan for her to see, to [Queen] Elizabeth I. Why did you pick that lifetime to show her?

J: That lifetime was significant in her spiritual evolution. Sometimes one friend is all you need in a lifetime, and that love can sustain you for many lifetimes.

N: That's so beautiful. With that, what were you trying to tell her about her life now?

J: That it's okay to be on your own. It's okay to have a few good friends when all around you others have many parties with many friends and many people. This is not always authentic. These people are not always true friends. It's better to stick to those true friends than have many false ones.

N: I'd like to ask about J's body and what it needs at this time most to optimize her health.

J: Rest. Rest is important. Even when you think you've had enough rest, sometimes lying down is all the medicine you need. Turning off from that which disrupts your mental state is also important.

N: It's a way to rest the mind, isn't it?

J: Yes. Too busy. Too much. Too much that's unable to be controlled.

N: Like information that might not be beneficial to her?

J: Yes. That information that's false, that creates fear, and false narratives that take up too much mental energy and disrupt the mental and hysical systems.

N: How would you suggest she sets boundaries with these other sources of information?

J: Leaving devices at home. Spending more time outside without them. Spending more time off the computer than on.

N: And how will this add to her life if she does this?

J: It would decrease negative mental energy, while increasing wellness.

N: What would be the best way for J to develop her psychic skills to their higher potential?

J: There are many ways in which to enhance psychic skills, but practice is needed. Nothing will come without practice, and sitting down daily to do that is the best way to trust the messages coming through.

N: How would you recommend she practices?

J: Sit in stillness for half an hour every morning and ask for a message. Write this message down without question, and do this every day.

N: Yes, I love that. What will it take for her to be able to do that? Is there anything that would assist her in making that commitment to herself?

J: Discipline. Ignoring all other impulses in the morning. Spending time to do that before anything else. This will become a habit after some time.

N: Beautiful. Is there anything else you can share about how to deepen psychic skills?

J: Nature. Spend time in nature. Nature talks to you whenever you are with it. Talk to it as if it's another being, and always trust the messages you get. There's too much questioning and not enough trust.

N: Yes. Beautiful. J is curious about her place of origin. What can you share with her about her origin?

J: J's origin is a place far away on the other side of the galaxy. It is a small planet. It does not have a name. It's just letters and numbers. She originated there and goes back there.

N: How does she go back there?

J: In dreams, in spaces throughout the day. She lives there as she lives here.

N: Is that one of the places that she goes in guided meditations?

J: Sometimes. Sometimes those spaces are just a way for her body to integrate the information that's coming through without her brain interfering.

N: Is that the same thing as when she's lost time in her life?

J: Yes. The lost time has been in her younger years when she was more connected to her place of origin, and those lives would sometimes interact. She would slip in there, into the other life, back into this life more easily than now.

N: Tell me more about this planet. What is it like there?

J: It is a beautiful place. It is like Earth, yet we respect nature and animals more than we do here on Earth. All life, all beings, are created equal. There is no eating animals, killing animals. We live alongside animals.

N: Are the animals similar?

J: Yes. There are many cats here, big ones and small ones. All life is sacred here. That's why Earth is so hard, with so much destruction, and so many people who consider animals to be lesser than. This is hard for J.

N: What is the reason why she chose to come to Earth from this place?

J: To experience the opposite. For soul growth, you need to have friction, and friction only comes from circumstances in which we're unfamiliar. You cannot grow in surroundings that don't challenge you, and so this is what she's here for... to see this, see the opposite.

N: Has she had many lifetimes on Earth?

J: Yes. Short ones, mainly.

N: Is she starting to understand what she came here to understand?

J: Subconsciously. It's not yet fully realized. In time.

N: This will be something that she will come to realize in this lifetime?

J: Yes. This lifetime is growth for many souls. There is much change, hardship. Much change, and much change will cause that soul growth to accelerate over a shorter period of time than in other lifetimes.

N: Yes. Is there anything that J could contribute to this world that would make her feel like she's making a powerful difference?

J: Showing up authentically. This time, there is much falsity. Authenticity is the only thing that will make a difference. We live in an age of great deception, and in time, people will see the authenticity through the deception.

N: Yes. In terms of her business and her interest in nutrition, is that part of what she's meant to speak authentically about?

J: Yes. This is a start.

N: What should she focus on as her next move with this business?

J: Continuing to learn, to look for information, to grow her skills to be of greater service to those who are looking for true health as a source of their wealth in this lifetime. So many are ill. There is so much illness and people don't know where to start. Continuing to study, to look for new avenues to explore, is the best way to continue for now.

N: Is she meant to see clients with this work?

J: For the short term, yes.

N: So, would you say that the main focus is sharing information then?

J: Yes. Written information. Start putting it on a website, blogging, as a means to begin.

N: Are there any other areas besides nutrition she could consider looking into?

J: Energy medicine would be another good area to focus on. Learning energy medicine may lead to the ability to read the energy of clients, of food. Do those energies match? Would that energy of that food match the energy of the person eating that food? Would it enhance that? Decrease that? This would be a good place to start.

N: Amazing. It's a good tool for knowing what information is true or false too, isn't it?

J: Yes. There is much food that is devalued nutritionally and energetically.

It does not enhance the systems, the bodies, of the people on Earth.

N: Could you share what one of the reasons might be for having ovary problems in this lifetime?

J: It's been passed down from previous generations. This is a trauma-induced manifestation. Working through trauma, healing generational trauma, will help to resolve these in time. Much has been resolved already. Many energetic systems and energetic changes change our biology and are passed down genetically.

N: Are we able to give her some healing assistance with that right now? (Yes.)
Tell me what you're doing as you do that.

J: Sending energy in and around the pelvic area, and it's warming up. This helps to improve physical functioning. Genes change, and once trauma is addressed, genes revert to their original status.

N: Will she notice a difference after today?

J: Yes. Healing is lifelong. That healing has been commencing since she was born. She's meant to heal this line so that it travels back and forward.

N: That's beautiful, and you'll continue to assist with this healing?

J: Yes, that is our job.

N: Thank you. What about J's teeth? What is the purpose or cause of teeth issues for her?

J: This is a manifestation of a lack of feeling safe, of feeling the inability to relax into safety around her and feeling the need to control the outcomes. This is something that manifests physically as well as emotionally.

N: Yes. Where did this feeling of not being safe originate from?

J: This was a womb injury. This was a feeling from the beginning, from birth, of not being safe in the world.

N: What is the purpose for J experiencing this?

J: To learn how to learn to be safe. To find the safety is to let go of control of the outcomes of being unsafe. To not allow it to make your world small, to do things anyway and realize that the fears are not always real and that safety was always there.

N: Yes. In the background. Even if we can't see it all the time, right? (Yes.)
Is there more that J needs to do to manifest continued health with her teeth or is this something that we can clear for her now that she understands the message?

J: This can be cleared now.

N: Okay. Tell me about how you're doing that.

J: The energy is pouring into the mouth area to remove blocked energy, blocked meridians, moving in between teeth, along gum lines, around the tongue, relaxing, releasing, and healing.

N: Is J feeling or sensing anything as you heal this?

J: A warmth and a tingling inside along the gum line. A feeling of release.

N: Let me know whenever you're complete.

J: (Moments later) The session is complete.

N: Okay. Before we go, are there any last messages that you would like to share with J?

J: There are many messages we would like to share. The most important of all is that you are loved, you have always been loved and that you are doing a good job here at this time. You are where you need to be and there is no need to rush for everything will come together in right timing. Don't force. Just be.

Chapter 8: Our Otherworldly Abilities

Now that you have seen that many of us have been witches and potentially even "aliens" in our past and/or parallel lives, you are now well aware that the Higher Self gives us an expanded perspective that can show us that we are so much more than we think we are. We may even have powers and abilities that are not currently well known on Earth but were practiced in the past, albeit in secret. In my session with L, I discovered there are magical abilities far beyond what most people currently deem to be possible.

An intuitive person working in a typical "muggle" job, L doubted her ability to make a full-time living from her healing work. She occasionally offered energy healing to clients online but sometimes questioned her abilities. L was holding on to many reasons why she couldn't do more energy healing work and leave behind her other job, which she despised. The resulting session confirmed that she had extraordinary intuitive abilities that were even more special than either of us could have predicted, and she did not need to doubt herself at all.

N: What do you see?

L: First thing I saw was a pyramid, presumably in Egypt, and then I saw myself inside a temple.

N: What else do you see as you look around?

L: White columns. Pillars. An altar. A single room with a room off to the back, and there's torches attached to the walls. The lights are flickering.

N: What else is around you?

L: Stone. Lots of stone. And gold. I can see stone and gold. I think there's people in the other room. There's no one in this room. I'm just standing in the middle looking around.

N: How do you feel in this place?

L: Fine. Curious. I can hear talking, whispering from others in the other room. I feel like they're walking towards me. They're walking down a little corridor. There's three of them. They walked into the room, and they're looking at me.
"Welcome." They said, "Welcome"... or they thought [it to] me telepathically, "Welcome."
The middle one stepped forward with their arms out, trying to hold my hands. "Welcome."
I feel like they've been waiting for me. I don't know what I'm doing there, but they know. And they've got smirks of, "Yes, we know why. It's okay that you don't know, but we know."

N: Can they tell you why you're here?

L: For healing and for training.

N: Training for what?

L: What's next.

N: Training for what's next?

L: I feel like it's... not to say an initiation... but I feel it's going to be some sort of, I don't know, crown chakra or third eye chakra kind of opening, and then I get a whole bunch of information, and whatever other healing is necessary, and then we go from there.

N: Who are these people?

L: The goddesses.
   Oh, I am stunned by that answer, but I don't know which goddess it is. They just said they're the Goddess.

N: As you look down at the ground, can you see your feet?

L: They're covered by my robes.

N: What do the robes look like?

L: A nice white, soft, flowy material that goes all the way to the ground.

N: Do you have any jewelry or ornaments on your body?

L: Gold bangle on my left wrist, and there's a gold headband around my forehead. My robe has a hood. I've got the hood up. I feel like I have long, long curly hair.

N: Does your body feel male or female? (Female.)
   Young or old?

L: Probably what I would equate to being in my early twenties. Kind of youngish, but adult.

N: How does this body feel? Does it feel healthy?

L: Ah, so good. It feels thin. It feels vibrant! I feel tall. It feels good.

N: Amazing. So, what do you feel you're meant to be doing next in this place?

L: I have to go with them into the other room. I don't know if it's going to happen or if it already has happened, but I've got a big goldish-whiteish energy cone on top of my head that's pointing toward my crown chakra.

N: And this is energetic? (Yes. Energetic.)
  What are they having you do next?

L: I'm sitting on the floor in the middle, and they're around me with their hands towards me, guiding or guarding or doing the energy stuff. And I'm looking at it from a different perspective. I can see myself there, but I'm seeing the whole room as if I was standing on the wall, and there's the cone thing, and it's like there are codes and symbols and whatever in goldy-white color appearing and coming down into the cone that's then feeding down into me.

N: Can you recognize any of those symbols? (No.)
  How does this feel?

L: Fidgety. Like my body is... I can't sit still. It's lots of energy and electricity or whatever you want to call it. I physically feel like I can't keep my body still.

N: Is it energizing?

L: Yes, that's the word. Yep.

N: What do you think it's doing for you?

L: It's giving me information and knowledge, and I feel a big sense of anticipation and excitement. And I can see... (Opens eyes)

I had to open my eyes because it was getting a bit much. When I close... (Closes eyes)

Oh wow... it's like there are flashes of light constantly all around the place, and it's quite intense. And then, when I opened my eyes, there was none of that. It was normal, nothing flashing around me. But when I close my eyes again, it's just light going all around the place.

And I feel like I'm getting information and instructions and all that kind of stuff. I don't know what it is, but I know I'm getting it.

N: Do you feel like you have been waiting for this day for a while? (Yes.)
Did you know it was coming?

L: I think deep down, yes. Or I was at least really, really hopeful.

N: What happens next?

L: I've stood up, and they're telling me that everything... (Suddenly changes subject)

I feel like I've gone invisible. My body's invisible.

I feel like if you go into a toy shop and you just have to try all the things all at once. "What does this do? What does this do? What does this do?" And it's like suddenly getting the knowledge that, yes, I know how to be invisible. "Oh, sweet. Turn that on." Bang, I'm invisible.

And then I come back, and suddenly I'm green, and I've got a different body. From my eyes up, I'm still there, but from the bridge of my nose, that's where I went invisible. But then I had this weird green body, and I can change.

I've discovered that I can change the way I look. I can change the way I look, and all these skills and talents and knowledge and whatever else... it's like it's all in my brain, in my head, in my energy, whatever. And it'll all present itself when it's needed.

And I feel a bit frustrated because I'm like, "Why can't I consciously know what all [my special abilities] are?" But the answer I got was, "You have all the things. So, if there's something you want to be able to do or to know or whatever, you just have to know that you've got all the things. There's nothing that you don't have." So, even though I would like to look at a list of things that I downloaded and be like, "Oh cool, I can be invisible. Yeah, I'll give that a shot." It's more a case of, "Wow, I wish I could be invisible right now." Bang, I know how to do it. It's done.

So, I've got all the things. I have to know that I have all the things, not doubt that I have something. Just know that I have all the things there, but even when I need something, I've got it.

N: What do you feel like doing next?

L: Going somewhere else. Completely.

N: Tell me about it.

At this point, L brings herself into a completely different lifetime without my prompting.

L: I feel like I'm in a field. Grass, or something that's like grass. Big open field, just walking through grass. But it's not Egypt. It's lush, it's thick grass, mid-calf height. And I'm just walking around.

There's people, there's mountains over there, with some trees. It's a clear, blue sky day. I don't think I'm carrying anything. Maybe a small bag over my shoulder. I'm just walking.

N: Are you a different person than you were before?

L: I'm a different person. I'm going to a new village because I walked up to the edge of the grass and I looked down, and there was a seaside village. And I'm going to start a new life in the seaside village, and I'm really excited.

N: Tell me more about what you're wearing.

L: Brown leather stuff. Boots and trousers. I think I might be a boy with long hair. And a shirt, but it's a tunic thing. My arms and everything are covered, but I feel like I've got a few layers on my top half.

N: Is this body young or old? (Young.)
How does this body feel? Is it healthy?

L: Very, very, very vibrant. Full of energy, full of enthusiasm, and wonder and excitement. The kind of kid that could run all day long if they needed to.
[I'm] going to find somebody. I'm going to be an apprentice.

N: An apprentice. Doing what?

L: Magick.

N: Is that why you're going to this town?

L: Yes, because there's an old man there I'm supposed to meet, but he's also a silversmith, blacksmith, some sort of thing like that. I can see him making tools with metal. So, I get to learn that as well as all the magick stuff.

N: Tell me about the place where you're learning about this.

L: There's just an ordinary-looking house in the village, which is next to the coastline. I don't think people know that he does that. People just know him as the silversmith or whatever. They don't know he does everything else. It's like a need-to-know basis. Nobody there needs to know... except for me, of course.

N: How did you find out about him?

L: I don't know. I just knew.

N: You felt called?

L: Yep. And he knows I'm coming. There's a bird. A bird told me. Big black bird.

N: Did you have magickal abilities before coming to this place?

L: I think I was just intuitive, and I knew I had to go after the bird. He sent me the bird, or he sent the bird to look for his next apprentice, and the bird found me, and I knew to follow the bird.

N: Tell me about your upbringing, where you came from, before going to this place.

L: I was in a village in a forest that was nothing spectacular. It was just a village in a forest, not a very dense forest. Just a village in a forest. So, people just did what they did and survived, traded whatever.

N: Does your family still live there?

L: I think so.

N: How do they feel about you leaving? Do they know?

L: Not sure. I don't feel sadness at leaving, and I don't feel like I'm carrying any sadness or missing anyone. All I'm thinking about is what's coming, what I'm getting to learn. I think it feels like they're like, "Oh well, there you go. That's one less mouth to feed, so that's kind of handy." You know, there are pluses and minuses to it. It feels very exciting.

N: Tell me about your studies and what the old man is showing you.

L: Showing me how to work with the metal, how to heat it, how to bend it, how to hit it, how to shape it, how to understand it, to know it, to know what it wants to do. Like, which piece of metal, whatever it is, would make the best sword for that person or which piece of metal would make the best chopping knife for that person. Which bit of metal would make the nicest cut for that person. So, it's learning, tuning into the metal to know what it wants to do because it's not an inanimate object. It has a consciousness and feeling… (Yawns), and all that sort of stuff, and I need to learn to listen to it.

N: Yes. (Picking up on the yawn.) Is this hard work?

L: It's hard work in the sense that it's long hours, but it's not physically taxing, and it's not mentally taxing. It feels like it lights me up all day, and I could go on all day and all night.

N: Amazing. What else does the old man teach you about?

L: I heard the phrase, "The ways of the universe and the nature of things." As in… everything has a consciousness that you can tap into. You can talk to the trees, you can talk to the air, you can talk to the ocean, you can talk to the Earth, you can talk to your house. Just got to learn how to connect to whatever it is that you want to connect to, but also understand that because that thing, whatever, tree has its own consciousness, it might not want to talk to you. So, you have to know the difference between you not finding the right frequency, but also the tree or whatever saying, "Not today," or "Not ever," or whatever.

N: Mmhmm (affirmative), respecting it. Honoring it.

L: Yes, because the tree may ignore you, but you may try and push it because you think you can't tune in, but it's actually just the tree ignoring you, so you need to learn the differences.

N: And do you have success with this knowledge, with using it?

L: I've learned that the trees are grumpy, but I'm better talking to the ocean. Even though I like trees better than the ocean.

N: They're just not as talkative?

L: Yep. I think they're annoyed at the people in general.

N: That makes sense. (Thinking about how humans cut so many trees down for their own use)

L: But the ocean's so big and so vast, it sees so much more than what the trees see, and the ocean's just like, "Yeah, cool, let's chat." Whereas the trees are like, "Bugger off, I'm a grumpy old tree."

N: What kinds of things does the ocean say to you?

L: The ocean is very... philosophical, I guess the word might be. It'll say things like, "The tides come and go. Everything's constantly changing."

Even if the change is so minute, everything is changing, and not all change is bad. Because if you want the low tides so that you can go out and collect crabs, you can't have a low tide all the time because you need a high tide to come in and replenish whatever. And then other people in other parts of the world need to have a low tide so they can get their food.

It's give and take, and you can't have everything all the time. You can't have the sunlight all the time because then the plants will die from too much sun. They need to have a rest just like people. So, we need the nighttime and the daytime, the outward tide and the inward tide.

And I feel like if I had a bad day or I'm grumpy or, you know, had a bad day for whatever reason, I'd go down to the ocean. I'd be like, "I'm so mad at blah blah blah blah blah." And the ocean would say, "Doesn't matter. You are the only one being hurt by somebody. This anger is only affecting you, it's not affecting the other person."

You're angry because you think that other person has wronged you or whatever, but the other person's not angry, the other person's not sad, the other person's not upset. You're only hurting yourself by your anger. Yes, it's a very valid emotion to feel, but hanging onto it is bringing you pain as well. So, release it. You've felt it. You've experienced it. You've acknowledged it. Okay, get rid of it. You don't need to hang on to it. (Sighs)

You don't need to validate yourself in your feelings by hanging onto emotions longer than the length of time to just recognize it in the first place. Does that make sense?

N: Yeah. It's like, "Get the message and let it go."

L: Yes. Like, "Oh, you've noticed you're angry. Okay, cool." That's the extent of what we need. Don't need to hang on to it. We don't need to have arguments in your mind about it. We don't need to roleplay different scenarios of what you could have said or how it could have gone. You've recognized the anger, you've gone, "Yes, I acknowledge I'm angry."

That's the extent of it. That's all you need. And then you can let it go. The rest of it is just causing pain.

N: And how does the boy take this information into his life? How does this relationship with the ocean benefit him?

L: It's like I know the feeling... I don't know the words. It's like the person that you go to because they always tell it straight, even though it's never what you want to hear. I want my feelings validated, and then the ocean says, "You've validated them. What do you want me to validate them for? I'm not going to baby you just because you want to feel angry. I've told you, 'Yes, acknowledge your anger.' That's all you need to do. Then, release it. You come to me for comfort and all of that, but I tell it to you straight. If you don't want to hear my straight answer, then go and talk to somebody else."

And then I get in a huff, and I walk away, and I'm like, "Damnit, the ocean's right." So, it's the person you go to for advice even though it's never what you want to hear, and they don't baby or indulge you. They just tell it how it is. You realize the truth of it. I feel like I'm immature, emotionally immature, in this lifetime, and I'm learning emotional maturity... as well as everything else.

N: So, it's like nature is your friend?

L: Yes, yes. In the 15-minute break (speaking about the time before the session started), I pulled a card, and I was like, "What's the biggest thing I'm gaining out of this?" And I got the card that said "Nature." I'm like, "Alright, cool." And now, yes, nature is my friend!

N: Can you speak with any other elements of nature?

L: No, I look at the trees. I look at them all the time, every day, but I don't go and talk to them. (Speaking of her current lifetime)

But I love looking at them because we're surrounded by trees here and there. I've always loved forests, but I don't talk to the trees. It's time to learn the lessons of the trees. I wasn't ready to learn the lessons of the trees in that life, so I learned the lessons of the ocean. I just needed a reminder. Now I can learn the lessons of the trees.

N: And you still have the same ability?

L: I just have to learn how to tune in and understand that not every single tree is going to want to talk to me, and have patience because it may not happen straight away because my ego gets into play.

N: Will it be easy once you can get out of your head? (Yes.)
And how will a relationship with the trees benefit you?

L: It will help anchor in... amongst other things... it will help anchor in abundance. Because trees have been coming to me for a while, since before we moved here over a year and a half ago, about the trees and the messages that they hold regarding abundance. Because a tree never says, "Oh, I think I have enough leaves. I'll stop growing my leaves so that the tree over there can grow leaves." It doesn't do that. Each tree has an infinite number of leaves, and its ability to grow leaves does not impact any other tree's ability to grow leaves.

And I've known before we lived here that I need to be surrounded by trees, and now I am. And now it's time to learn about... it's time to talk to the trees. And it's abundance, it's grounding, because trees can withstand wind, rain, and hurricanes. Trees can withstand bad weather because they have strong roots and they have strong footing.

And sometimes even with trees, some trees even need fire to regenerate. Some trees need to be burnt up so that they can regenerate. And my mom keeps harping on me lately because we're surrounded by trees. She's paranoid about bushfires and everything burning down. A year or so before we moved here, I kept imagining someone coming in and burning everything down and then I start again. I don't want to actually have everything burned down because that would be annoying. But energetically, [I'm] going to rise up from the ashes now because I feel like everything has burned down. Now I get to rise up from the ashes. Another lesson of trees.

N: And this is metaphorical?

L: Yes. I really would not like an actual bushfire in my house. My mum is legitimately worried about bushfires. I am surrounded by bush. But yeah, this is all metaphorical, energetic, not literal.

I have to talk to the trees to understand the rising from the ashes, and the nature of abundance, and the nature of really good grounding because you need to have big roots in order to rise up. So, if I want to grow my spiritual connections, I need to be really grounded. Otherwise, I'll fall over.

N: What are some practices you can do to feel more grounded? What do the trees say?

L: Actually be outside with the trees. Ask the trees for help. Remember to do it more often, because my grounding practice is not that great. So, it's like you have to remember to do this every day, all the time, all the time.

Be grounded so that you can withstand whatever comes, and so that you can grow big and tall and strong. Whatever you want to do, you have to have good grounding, but I need to do it a lot more often.

N: Yes. What else can you do to expand your spiritual intuition, powers, abilities?

L: Don't decide that it's going to be hard or that it has to happen now. Just get out of your head. Get out of my head and allow. And I had an example of that the other night and it was great. It was wonderful. It was something I'd been asking for three years and I got it, and it was completely out of the blue. And the message I got was that I'm also really caught up in my emotions. Like I fester in my emotions and this is another reminder from the ocean.

I fester in my emotions and I let them take over me, whereas I need to practice releasing them once I acknowledge their existence. That's all. Release, release, release, release. I fester way too long. The festering in my emotions locks a lot of things because my grandma [in spirit] came to me the other night, and she said she couldn't come sooner because my grief would overtake me and prevent me from being in that moment with her.

And it happened. I was balling my eyes out knowing that she'd come. She's like, "See, I didn't want to upset you," but I let my grief get the better of me or I let my anger get the better of me or I let my frustration or whatever other emotion I'm going through, I let it get the better of me. So that when I sit and I'm like, "I need help with this," and I'm festering in anger, I can't hear a response. So, I need to practice more with releasing the emotion and clearing the emotions out so that I can hear the response.

N: Yes. And is it the tree telling you these things or you're just sort of realizing them?

L: The combination. I feel like part of me is here with the trees that are surrounding me and part of me is in that lifetime looking at the trees that are surrounding the village and everybody's having realizations all at once and it's feeding through.

L's session is a beautiful example of a session in which the client already possesses psychic abilities without the need for hypnosis. Being under hypnosis, however, revealed even more abilities than she had even realized were possible. Notice how she seems to be joining in on the conversation as if she, her human self, is very present in the conversation. From here, I call forth L's Higher Self to ask follow-up questions on why these specific visions have appeared to her.

N: I know the Higher Self could have brought forth many different lifetimes for L to see today. You chose to bring forward the woman in the Egyptian temple getting the energy downloads. Why did you pick that lifetime to show her?

L: Because it's another reinforcement of belief. Believe that you have everything already and have unwavering belief in the universe. Unwavering belief in the God... God figure.

N: Yes. And are those powers still inside of her now?

L: Yes. They may have become dormant or covered over due to a belief that we needed additional reminders to help her believe.

N: Yes. And how will believing help her in her life now?

L: She'll have faith that things will be better. With the faith comes a change of attitude and a change of beliefs and a change of thoughts. Once all of those change, the reality that she lives in will change.

N: Yes. How could her reality change?

L: In every way. If she thinks, "This could be better. Let's change it to this, or it should be changed to this..." if she believes it's possible, it'll change.

N: Absolutely. Is there anything else you're trying to show her about her life now through that life?

L: She's more powerful than she believes, but we will not give her all the answers. She must go through the process of finding them herself. It's not our place to just tell her or anyone because then what is the lesson for the lifetime if you just get told? The lesson of the lifetime is to learn and experience and grow and try... not just be told.

N: What can L do to tune in to receive these answers for herself?

L: Stop talking.

N: Anything else?

L: That will be hard enough. There are many ways to listen. Some days it might be listening, some days it might be meditation, some days it might be writing, some days it might be just a shower. There are many ways to listen. The key point is to stop talking.

N: Okay, listen more. What about the lifetime of the young man going to the seaside village to apprentice? Why did you pick that lifetime to show her?

L: Although tools are wonderful, we have everything we need in nature. Because the tool itself, the sharpness of the blade, the length of the blade doesn't matter. The consciousness of the steel working with the consciousness of the person is what matters. Anything can be fixed or cut or whatever the purpose of the tool is. Many, many things can do it, but it's the consciousness of the item and the consciousness of the person just as it is the consciousness of the water with the person or the trees or the flower or the apple; it's about building connections. You don't need to have a candle or a herb or a knife or a cup. You need a consciousness and a connection.

N: Yes. And what were you trying to tell her about her life now through that piece of wisdom?

L: She's looked at so many answers inside of herself when there are many consciousnesses around her that she can work with. There are many trees, many types. There is her dog, there's the land in general, there is the air consciousness that she can work with, and when she opens to that, a lot more consciousness comes forward.

N: Yes. So she doesn't have to do all the healing on her own, does she? A lot of it is about working with the energy and listening. (Yes.)
    And not worrying about the outcome ahead of time.

L: The opportunity to live in this space [on this property] does not come by accident. The land and the trees want her just as much as she wants them.

N: And why do they want her?

L: Because her energy in this area can elevate. And they wanted someone to elevate rather than someone to pull it down.

N: Yes. And how is she elevating the area?

L: Bringing in knowledge and wisdom and practices that have been long missed in this area. The land, the spirits had not had a human to work through for a long time and wanted to call in someone who can work with them so that the land benefits as well as the human does.

N: Beautiful. Is there anything else you'd like her to know about the land?

L: It's far more supportive and wants her success more than she currently comprehends. There is a lot to benefit for her in this area. She just has not tapped into it.

N: Yes. But now she knows how to do that.

L: And that she should. And the longer she puts it off, the longer it'll take to reap the benefits that she so desires.

N: Because they work as a symbiotic relationship, would you say?

L: Yes. Everyone benefits. Everyone's waiting. The trees are ready, the land is ready. We're just waiting for L to be ready. L is ready. She has been putting it off because she was afraid of what it might mean to feel her abundant self or her successful self because she's not experienced it in this lifetime. And the potential experience of something new, even though desired, is still surrounded by fear and uncertainty.

N: Yes. Only because it hasn't happened before. Is there anything that she actually needs to fear? (No.)
 So, what about healing other people? What direction should L take in her healing work for people?

L: Whatever direction she chooses. There are many paths open, but her head in the sand is blocking her view of the paths. Some paths may be more successful than other paths, but each path would hold a lesson. No path is better or worse than the other. It's just an experience to be had. She may choose to continue on that experience or choose to change it to a different experience.

N: Her beliefs matter a lot in that, don't they?

L: They do.

N: Is healing even something that L's meant to continue doing?

L: She's meant to if she chooses it.

N: She has a choice.

L: She always has a choice. She doesn't believe she has a choice. She believes that choices are made by those outside of her and all the choices are within. She doesn't like the choices that she makes or she lets circumstances make the choice for her. Even though circumstances allowed multiple choices, she just let the circumstance and the choice of others become her choice.

N: Why does she do that?

L: It's what she's always done in this lifetime.

N: So, it's just a pattern and a conditioning.

L: Yes. She's not experienced an opportunity to choose her own path and be fully supported in that. She's been presented with, "This is the choice you will make and this is the only option for you," and had to deal within that.

N: Yes. How can she make different choices and feel empowered that she has some control over those choices?

L: By having belief. Belief in the universe, belief in God/the Goddess, belief in herself, belief in her own power and her own energy... and if she believes the world is conspiring to help her even in tough situations, then it will. If she believes the world is out to get her down, then it will. If she believes she has no power in choices, that's what will manifest. If believes she can get herself to create any reality she chooses, then that's what will manifest.

But at present, her head is in the sand because her belief is that other people's choices are more important and her choices don't matter. So, she has given up making choices because they don't matter anyway. So, when she asks, "What do I do? What do I do? I don't know what to do." She doesn't know how to make a choice.

N: She can do whatever she wants to do.

L: She just has to remember she can and that she can choose to make a choice.

N: Yes. Amazing. Related to that, L was confused about how she could express the idea that we actually choose our life experiences to her clients - which is interesting given this conditioning that she herself is experiencing. Could you share anything around that?

L: L can choose to work with clients for whom that belief is a part of them anyway. If she chooses to work with clients or people in her healing work that go against that belief, then it'll be infinitely harder. If she chooses to work with clients that share her belief system, even just to a small extent, life will be infinitely easier in that regard because the choice would've already been made in that she chooses to work with people who already understand that.

N: Yes. Is it just a block that she's sort of creating for herself out of fear?

L: There is that fear because in her past experiences she has not seen success. She has not seen flow, she has not seen that ease. It's hard to choose those parts when you have not seen it before. But she will. The hardest part and the most fearful part is around making different choices.

N: Yes, but she knows now that she can choose differently.

L: She does deep down.

N: How long will it take for her to embrace this?

L: That is up to her to choose. This can be an easy lesson or this can be a hard lesson. The choice is hers. She has to make a choice and stick to it. This is a process of complete rewiring of underlying beliefs. The underlying belief is having faith and having trust in the universe, God, Goddess, whatever terminology she chooses to use, having faith in her soul, having faith in herself. Once she has that, all other choices come easily.

N: Yes, and hearing this today will help her, won't it?

L: It will. Although none of it is new information to her because if she stopped talking, she would've known the answers anyway.

N: Well, now she'll be able to hear it in a more concrete way, which you know us humans seem to need for some reason.

L: I believe she'll listen to this [recording] often.

N: Wonderful. How can L make more money?

L: Choosing to. She may believe that there are many blocks in her path to creating all that she desires in her life, but it is simply a choice. She chooses to believe that she will not get paid [well] for her position. She chooses to believe that no other positions [will arise] that will meet all of her needs.

She chooses to remain bound to her current position and her current boss because it is easier to remain working at home and it is easier to play the victim of a small income. She has not experienced being able to choose a higher income because this has not been a part of her reality in this lifetime because of the beliefs and choices of others that she has taken on.

N: Has she had other lifetimes where she was able to support herself more easily?

L: There have been lifetimes where she has done that and there have been lifetimes where she has done that and it was taken away. She has made efforts to heal those lifetimes. She has not yet revisited the lifetimes where she has had it and maintained it.

N: Yes. So, it's about anchoring in that vision more than the others that could change this?

L: Yes. She's more focused on finding what is wrong than finding what is right.

N: What will she be able to do when she allows herself to choose to make more money?

L: She can experience ease and expansion in ways she's never experienced before. She can feel more joy than she's experienced before. She can feel a new level of intimacy in her marriage that she hasn't before.

N: So, it's a positive choice for her to make for herself.

L: It's a very positive choice.

N: Beautiful. Should she keep her current job... if that's the choice she wants to make for herself?

L: She may keep it until something else changes. She understands the timing and the nature of which she works. She understands that if this change was to happen tomorrow, she would not leave her job due to the nature of the work - and because she's a kindhearted person who puts the nature of the work ahead of her - but that is not to her detriment at the moment. That is just nature of a kind person. If this were to change after her birthday, everyone may have a different conversation because the nature of her work, timing of her work, will have changed. So, she may feel free to choose alternative employment with a clean conscience.

N: So, it's okay to change. It will be okay for her to change her job.

L: It'll be okay for her to change her job tomorrow. She'll just feel guilt. That is because she understands the nature and timing of [her] role with deadlines and whatnot and the amount of work [that's] on currently, and there are other things at play that she's unaware of within her workplace. If she were to change her role in November, she would do so freely without guilt. It would be easier emotionally.

N: As she's looking for ways to replace that income and shift her energy into something else, can you give a hint or an idea of what she could focus on to work on her healing abilities and strengthening them for work?

L: She should work on believing that what she has to offer is worthwhile. Currently, she does not believe that, and until she does believe it's worthwhile, no one else will believe it's worthwhile. She could read testimonials and talk to previous clients and she will start to understand. But yes, she needs to believe that what she has is worthwhile. She believes that the work that she does is not deep enough or not thorough enough or not enough. She needs to believe that it is.

N: Yes. What does her healing work do for people?

L: It changes their lives. They may not see it straight away. L is currently thinking about a client that she worked on last year, over 12 months ago, and the results from that work are only now coming to fruition. L felt guilty that the results did not come sooner for her client who spent money on her services. L felt guilty that the results did not come sooner, but the results are here now or they're starting to take place now. But L cannot be the judge of when the results are due to come in because that is up to that person.

N: Her work is still valuable even if it takes a longer amount of time. (Yes.)
Is there a bigger benefit to it taking more time or is there a reason for that?

L: The person involved needed more time, needed more time to process, needed more time to understand what was at play, needed more time to be comfortable coming to the decision that was made.

N: So, she did her part, the client.

L: She did.

N: And that's what was important.

L: It is. It may have taken longer in days and weeks than what was desired, but that was how it played out for that person. Nobody can control the way a reality will play out for a person except for that person. L's work opens doors, moves mountains, clears drainage points. It is still up to that person to walk. L cannot push them physically or energetically.

N: They have to make their own choices just as she does.

L: That's right.

N: What benefit does she get from doing the healing work for other people besides money?

L: It creates an expanding understanding of the universe of energy, consciousness as a whole. She has seen examples of how actions she takes now are connected to actions with people from the beginning of time. She has seen examples of the interconnectedness of everything, the energies and locations and lifetimes that she works with, in varying clients, serves as curiosity and an education for her so that she can understand more about the universe and of life, and the lives that we live, and the nature of humanity, and the nature of spirits, and the nature of the universe.

N: It's so much bigger than a business, isn't it?

L: It is. It is... a goal... it is a plan for the lifetime to learn about the nature of the universe presented by operating a business. Because what better example of the nature of the universe than real life examples. It is preferred for her to work with that rather than learning from a book.

N: So, it's not really about the money deep down, is it?

L: It is not. There are lessons that come from the money and there are joys and benefits from the money, to be sure, that go far and beyond the meeting of the physical needs. But the ultimate goal is to understand the nature of reality for the universe in which we live and the way that everybody interacts with it.

N: Yes, and is running the business and doing healing the best way for her to learn about that then?

L: Most likely. She could learn from interacting with people, from talking to people, but as her life presents it at the moment, and the area in which she is, [she] would be better off working in the healing space to attract those who are like-minded from all around the world as opposed to just her local area. She could choose to understand the nature of reality and she does by talking to people, getting to know people. However, she's currently learning that there are many that do not share her belief systems and that is limiting for her and her experiences. She would be better served by interacting with those that share her belief system or belief systems that match in whatever way they match, allowing cultural differences and whatnot. Basically, she would be better off interacting with those that have a belief in spiritual principles rather than not.

N: Is working online a good way for her to find those people?

L: It is because then she can reach all around the world. There are other areas within her local area, but her belief is currently that people would not travel that far to see her in person. So, that choice is up to her.

N: It's up to what she chooses to believe.

L: It is. If she chooses to believe people will travel, she will find people that will travel. If she chooses to believe online is the best way, then the online will be the best way. If she chooses to let the universe decide how to bring clientele in, then guess what? People will come.

N: Yes. And she has to believe in that too, doesn't she?

L: She does, but she understands. She's seeing the humor in this.

This portion of L's session is a great reminder that, even though there is a plan for your life that your Higher Self made, we still have the free will to make our own choices within that plan. We get to choose what we do with the circumstances that are provided.

Many people often wonder about the dichotomy between free will and destiny. L's Higher Self illustrates how these two sides of the coin work together in tandem. There is the greater plan, and then there are the smaller choices we make along the way that may alter or elevate that plan.

The Higher Self can always edit the plan from the other side according to our human choices, just like the human self can decide if they want to listen to their higher guidance or take a different route instead. The planning process between the soul and the personality is malleable and adaptable all throughout life. The session continues...

N: I'd also like to ask about the dream that L recently had about *The Last Unicorn*. Could you shed some light on the reason for that dream?

L: It was a dream that was meant to instill in her a sense of wonder and excitement that she is, in fact, a healer. That her healing skills are unmatched for those that she is bound to be working with in this lifetime. They're in fact unmatched compared to any other on this planet because every healer's skills are unmatched to every other healer. That's why we have so many healers, and that's why we need healers. Everyone's skills are unmatched to everybody else. She needed a sense of wonder and excitement that she was destined to be a healer.

N: Amazing. So, that's good confirmation for her listening back that, yes indeed, healing is meant to be her path and it's up to her to choose how she wants to do that in a way that works best for her. (Yes.)

N: I'm curious about L's skin flare-ups. Are we able to give her some information about where that comes from?

L: Where it comes from is not as relevant anymore because it is the past and it cannot be changed. What is relevant is going forward and allowing herself to present differently.

She has identified as a person with bad skin, as the person with the red face, as the person who needs to cover it up, as a person who needs to treat it. That has formed part of her identity.

Whilst she believes that all of the options haven't worked, [the] point is that she believes that they haven't worked. She believes that the spray she's currently using is working, but very slowly. If she believed that it worked very quickly, she may see different results.

She also believes that if it worked quickly it would clear up, but then it would come back. If she believed that she could clear it up once and for all, then she could clear it up once and for all. The spray that she's currently using is effective and could be made more effective by a change of formula of which she does have access to. We can show her that at a later time should she wish. She will be able to determine the ingredients through the use of muscle testing.

She needs to believe that it can be cleared quickly and easily and once for all, but she has to also release it out of her identity so she no longer identifies as the person with a bright red face. But again, she has not had many opportunities in this current lifetime to identify as a person with nice skin or as the clean skin, shall we say.

L is also undergoing a very big transformational process in that she's releasing identities and coming to terms with creating new ones, but as none of these are things she's currently experienced in this current lifetime, it is made more difficult. She has no basis to believe in.

She would do well to seek out further past lives where she has succeeded abundantly, where she has succeeded with clear skin, where she has succeeded in all the things that she desires so she can have a conscious knowledge of what it feels like to have those things. When she has felt what it feels like to have nice skin, it does not need to be covered up with foundation. It does not need to be covered in creams and sprays and it will be much easier for her to clear that identity out of her current belief system.

N: So, are you saying that by almost over-obsessing over the issue and tending to it so much that it reinforces the belief? (Yes.)

Interesting.

L: Just as looking at your hair everyday saying, "I have brown hair," or "I have green eyes," reinforces that, and if you were to change your hair color, it would look strange until you got used to it. It's the same principle, it's just that nobody thinks about it in terms of hair color or eye color or the nail color that they choose at the salon. It is all the same.

N: Yes. So, to change her beliefs, it's just a choice to change them.

L: It is. And a time allowed to get used to the change.

N: How can she create a practice of shifting her beliefs in a way that's grounded and consistent?

L: There are multiple ways she could do this. She could put post-it notes up. She could create a meditation track for herself. She could pay attention to the thoughts that she thinks about when she's absentmindedly thinking and she could change them in the moment. There would be her three best options.

N: Yes. The physical reminders seem to help us humans since our minds are very busy most of the time.

L: Yes, she will do well being mindful of thoughts that creep up on her and she thinks about without realizing, being more mindful of her thoughts.

N: Yes. And with teeth issues and weight loss, are those other areas that can shift through her beliefs as well?

L: Yes. We're hesitant to say yes because she's expecting instant results and it would not serve her to have instant results because she would not change the underlying patterns. If she were to believe that tomorrow she woke up and all issues with her teeth resolved, she would not change and work on the underlying patterns that created the issues in the first place. If she was to wake up tomorrow being thin and in the body she desired, she would not continue to endeavor to become more fit physically by exercise, whereas that is necessary.

N: The process has value. Amazing. Can we go ahead and do a body scan looking through all of the areas of L's body and just let us know if there's anything else we need to be aware of and just do a scan, from the top of the head to the bottom of the feet, and let us know if there are any problems or anything that might be out of balance that we haven't talked about yet.

L: At this moment, there is not.

N: Okay. Could we give her some healing just generally today?

L: Of course.

N: Let me know what you're doing as you do that.

L: We are, as you would say, opening the taps, letting the flood of excess leave her energy body and her mind.

N: How is L feeling as you do that?

L: She is understanding that this is a water energy going through her and that it is reinforcing the nature of the water energy, the lessons from the water that she has learned through other lifetime studies that we have been reinforcing now. (Pauses and sighs)

And she's having other realizations about water in her body and the excess of water in her body. There are realizations happening as well as energy healing.

N: Yes. Making connections. Amazing.

L: But with holding the water in her body and the puffiness that she experiences and she has said many a time that she holds onto water, the very nature of water and the lesson of the ocean is that it should not be held. Sometimes there is more, sometimes there is less. The flow is needed when she's experiencing puffiness and she's experiencing the withholding of water in her skin and in her tissues. This is a sign that she's withholding energy and emotions and thoughts that need to be released and the more she holds on, the more water she will hold onto because the water is the representation of our emotional state and her emotions in general.

So, this is a reminder for L, and the connection has been made that when she sees her fingers are puffy, she feels her throat and her neck is puffy. There are emotions that she needs to release. There are thoughts that she needs to release so she can allow the water in her body to move and to go freely as it should.

N: Yes. This has been an amazing session.

L: It's been a long time coming.

N: Before we go, are there any last messages you'd like to share with L while you have her attention?

L: Not right now. She knows that she will do well believing, and she knows that she will do well releasing. We can't force her to remember. It is up to her.

N: Thank you very, very much.

L: Thank you for the opportunity.

Chapter 9:
Healing Goddess Energy

Many spiritual people look up to gods, goddesses, angels, Ascended Masters, and other energies they deem to be "above" them in vibration. What if, at one point, we were gods and goddesses, and we have forgotten? What if we have already lived in those higher vibrational realms, or perhaps even other planets, and have chosen to come down to Earth to make our healing work more tangible on the human level?

It's already been demonstrated that we can bring extraordinary healing abilities in with us from other lifetimes. We also have powers and abilities that we have brought from other spiritual realms. This was the case with V, a client who regularly channels etheric entities in her energy healing and breathwork sessions.

V's story is especially interesting because her extrasensory abilities did not develop for her until much later in life. They hid beneath the surface, waiting for her to excavate and set them free. It wasn't until she began actively pursuing her healing journey in her forties and fifties that her intuitive abilities came in like an avalanche, surprising her and many others around her.

Although one does not need to be psychic to have an amazing hypnosis session, pre-existing intuitive abilities can create an even more heightened and in-depth awareness for a psychic person in a trance. They may receive visions of levels and dimensions that a typical person cannot access because of the unique experiences and mastery their soul has gleaned from these other realms.

It is often said that it is easier for psychics to channel answers for other people than it is to find answers for themselves. There can be a personal bias and desire to hear a particular answer come through that can get in the way of hearing clear answers for oneself. Hypnosis allows a client, whether psychic or not, to bypass this personal bias and provide themselves with clarity around the questions they have about their own lives as they connect to the wisdom of their Higher Self.

We may not realize just how spiritually advanced and powerful we are until we connect with our Higher Selves and discover more about the journey our soul has already been on, as we will see illustrated in V's session now.

N: What are you seeing, V?

V: A bright light.

N: What else are you seeing around you?

V: It's a vast area. It's almost like I'm in the clouds. And it's getting brighter, this white light.

N: Yes. Tell me more about what you're seeing.

V: I see people starting to gather around me. They're coming out from the clouds. They're coming in and wanting to see me and talk to me.

N: How do you feel in this place?

V: It's very peaceful.

N: Beautiful. Tell me about these people that are gathering around you.

V: There are some men and some women, and they're wearing the... you know like the Jesus garb... with a wrap around their shoulder and a rope belt. Even the women are in it.

N: Yes. Are they saying anything to you?

V: No. There's many of them coming out and they are just very happy to see me. There's one that's wanting to come a little closer and place his hand on my shoulder, and he is just talking like, "Dear child. We're so happy that you're here."

N: Beautiful. Is there anything else they want to show you?

V: I see a screen that's got a colorful [display]. It's moving fast... there are lifetimes that are moving... and it's in fast forward... of experiences and memories, and it's just playing. It's like I could push a button or touch the screen and it would pause on a scene.

N: Is there anything you feel drawn to look at on the screen?

V: It's moving so fast. It's almost like, on Instagram, how all the oracle cards go really, really fast, and if you screenshot it, that's your message of the day. (Chuckles)

N: So, it's just shuffling through images? (Yeah.)
    Beautiful. It's a beautiful place.

V: Yeah, they're just kind of, they're excited that I'm there and they're waiting on me to see where I'm going to touch the screen and pause the scene.

N: What else is happening?

V: It's just an enormous cloud, and some of the others have backed away. It's like they greeted me and then they bowed away. But I'm still standing there with… I think it's just the one with his hand on my shoulder.

N: Do you recognize any of these people?

V: No. No. They just look very peaceful and kind and welcoming. I think they're ready for me to push the screen. I can tell I'm a little nervous though to do that because… (Trails off)
But I trust I'll be shown what I need to see, so I'm just going to press it!

N: And did anything come up on the screen?

V: Light blues… blue and green. At first I thought it was yellow, but it landed on a blue and green screen.

N: Can you make out any images in the colors?

V: It's almost like green trees, and I guess it actually looks like a satellite view of the Earth where it's blues and greens or like when you're high up on an airplane or something and you're looking down.

N: It's a bird's eye perspective. (Yeah.)
Is anything else happening on the screen?

V: No. It's just like the bird's eye view of Earth. It's like I'm seeing things from where I am in the clouds. Maybe I can look over and see things from that perspective. So, now it's like I'm not looking at it through the screen. I'm looking at it off the cloud where I'm standing.

N: Yes. I'm going to help you find the most appropriate place to drift down off of the cloud.

At this point, I guide V to move slowly and gently down to the surface.

N: What are the first impressions that you have?

V: It's like a desert land, but it feels like another place, another planet. It looks like the desert, but it's not the desert. It's definitely another planet, but it's brown like a desert.

N: Yes. What else do you see as you look around?

V: There's nothing there. It feels like it used to be home, but now it's just one big empty planet. Nobody's there anymore.

N: Is there anything in the distance?

V: It just looks very sad, like a sad planet. It just has a sad energy to it. It used to be something, and now it's just desolate, and I feel like I used to be here. This used to be my home, and now I see that it's gone. It's just nothing. And I'm just having some memories of a war, and it used to be so beautiful.

N: Describe to me what it used to be.

V: It used to be... it feels like Atlantis when I'm having a flashback to the memories. It was everything I imagined Atlantis to be, where there's just lush land all around and beautiful people, and there's a lot of just joy and laughter and magic. People are using their hands to move things and they just are putting, moving things with their hands. (Deep breath) Just a lot of joy around there.

N: If you look down at your feet, what do you see?

V: At first I saw the lush land of what used to be, and then I remembered that it's brown. So, I switched back between the memory of lushness and the reality of what it is now. And I want to go back to where it's pretty when it was so easy and fun.

N: What are you wearing on your body?

V: I feel like I'm in that same [garb]... what everybody approached me with in the very beginning with the white robe with the shoulder exposed. But it feels like it's a little more fancy. It's a little more updated than what they had on up on the cloud.

N: Do you have any jewelry or ornaments on your body?

V: Yeah, there's gold. Everything's lots of gold and lots of white.
    And then everything's just so lush and green, and the waters are so blue, and I do feel like royalty. I do feel like I'm somebody special here. I am special. I have some good powers that are really helping to teach people.

N: Ooh. What about... are you carrying anything?

V: I don't think so, no. I'm just higher up on a mountaintop. My view is a little bit better so I can observe everyone, and it's almost like they come up to teach or up to learn. So, it's like I'm a little bit higher up on a mountain and people have to travel to come and see me, but it's worth the walk. It's worth the trek to get up there because they're going to receive so much.

N: Yes. What do they receive when they come to see you?

V: It almost feels like a blessing of sorts. All I have to do is touch them and it transforms. If I touch them on their forehead, it's like this golden light comes from my hand, and it just goes down their entire body. It's just a beautiful healing thing that, yeah, I just touch them and this golden light just goes down and clears out whatever is in their way, clears out all the density, all the stuff in their way. It clears a whole pathway, just floods their whole body with this beautiful golden light.

N: Amazing! Does your body feel male or female?

V: Female, definitely.

N: Young or old?

V: I guess... not too young and not too old. She's very beautiful, and she just holds herself with this wisdom and knowledge. She's not quite sixty. She's probably in her forties or fifties.

N: And how does this body feel? Does it feel healthy?

V: Very healthy, yes.

N: So, in the scene that we're watching, is it the time when the area is lush?

V: Yes. It's beautiful and I'm up on the mountain, and people travel up the mountain to come see me, and then when they're with me it's like they sit at my feet and I just place my hand on their forehead and it's like a healing activation of sorts.

N: How do you feel in this position?

V: It feels so beautiful because I'm helping so many people. It comes so easy to me. It doesn't take anything from me. I just so easily am able to share this, and it's almost like when I was up on the cloud... just the gentle touch of that hand on my shoulder... that felt so powerful. It's like I can just simply put my hand right there and it's just that easy.

N: Do the people who come to see you call you anything in particular?

V: Ma ma, they're calling me ma ma.

N: And do you live at the top of this mountain somewhere?

V: I do, yes, I do live up there. I go down the mountain because that's where things are fun. That's where I get to interact with everyone. But when I'm working...
 (Whispers to self) Not "working"... when I'm pouring into others in that way, it's up there.

N: Take me to the place where you live and look at the outside of it and describe it to me.

V: It's like it's one big open air palatial area. You know how you imagine Greek mythology... kind of like how it's got the columns and everything's open and yet covered? There's no walls, I guess. I think that's what I'm trying to say. (Yes.)
 So, it's very palatial but open and there's a beautiful breeze that is always there.

N: How do you go inside of this place?

V: It just feels like it's all one big open space. There's a main area that has the area where I sit and people line up to come sit in front of me. And then there's a separate area that is around the back, and those are kind of like my living quarters. There's my big beautiful bedroom. So, it's all one big space, but the front end is the healing space and then the backend is my living space.

N: Do you live with anyone?

V: I don't think so. It looks like I have some people helping me and supporting me, but I don't see a lover or anyone like that.

N: Okay. What is life normally like for you in this place?

V: It seems really beautiful. I spend my days working with people and healing with them and putting my hands on them. And then when I want to go down the mountain, and I want to be social and hang out, I get to do that. And if I just want to relax and go to bed or play at the water, I have the space to do that as well.

N: How did you come to take on this role?

V: I wonder... It feels like when I was on the planet, that planet, it's like I learned something up there, and then I was sent down to this land, to this beautiful lush land. So, it's like whatever I learned, I learned up there. I trained on [that] planet and then I went down to wherever this is.

It really feels like Atlantis area. I don't know if that's just the scene that it reminds me of or if that's actually what it was. But then when I go back to that planet, I realize that it's just not what it was when I was there and when I was trained. But that's where I learned everything was up there on that planet.

N: And then you're bringing it down. So, it was divinely orchestrated?

V: Yes. Yeah, it was definitely a plan. They were training me to go down and do that.

N: And do you feel like you're accomplishing all that you set out to?

V: Yes. Yes, I definitely do. It feels very peaceful. There are always people there that will come up, and it's like they just know when… I guess… maybe I have hours. Everybody just knows my hours and when they can come see me.

N: Beautiful. Let's go ahead and leave that scene and let's move forward to an important day, a day that you consider to be important. We've now moved forward to an important day. What's happening?

V: I feel like there was that same me, now I'm much older, and there is a lot of fighting and war going on all around me on this beautiful lush land, and things are not peaceful. People are not okay. There's just so much fighting and resistance.

N: And what are people fighting about?

V: I can't tell. But people that I love… that I know… my people that were originally there, they're running, and they're trying to go somewhere safe. And I just feel like it's definitely a takeover. Some negative agendas are coming in and trying to take over our beautiful land.

N: And how are you feeling about all of this?

V: I'm feeling very distressed. I'm feeling very out of control. I want so much to be able to help, and I'm just... I feel so frustrated. We've worked so hard to create this beautiful space, and there's been so much peace, and now it's just all disappearing right underneath my fingers.

N: What do you do?

V: I see myself having a cape of some sort, and it's like I get in a crouching down position and I pull the cape over me, and then I just disappear. I just go away. It's not even like I was murdered. It's like I was able to remove myself, but I don't know where I went. It was like a magic trick. I just pulled it over my head and knew that I was going to go when I did that, that I was going to be away. I wasn't going to be there anymore.

N: So, sort of how we would say passing away, but in your own way? (Yeah. Yeah.)

Okay. Let's go ahead and move forward and see where you end up. Where do you go after you disappear?

V: Well, it takes me back to the planet, though… that is now nothing and it's still nothing. So, it's like I don't know where I thought I was going to go, but now I'm me standing on this again.

It's like we're kind of looking at each other. "How'd you get here?" It's me standing there, but then this version of me just popped in there, too, and I'm looking at her and she's looking at me. "What are you doing here? How did we get here?" (Laughs)

At this point, V meets up with herself from a past life and communicates with that version of herself as her current human self.

N: Is there anything either of you feel called to share with each other?

V: She's saying that she's proud of me. She's saying that I have a lot of work to do and that I'm needed back down there and I have to go back.

N: What kind of work do you need to do?

V: She's just saying that you have... that we have... these powers that can really, really help people transmute their pain, that can help relieve their suffering. And just by being in our presence, we're able to help alleviate the resistance that people feel in their body. And she's saying that even though her work is done in that time, it's time for me to go back and do this in this time.

N: Yes. What do you think was the purpose of that lifetime?

V: It was just such a beautiful time of being, of experiencing, of magic, that we all got to witness within each other. It's like there was just so much beauty and joy and with the peaceful energies that everybody was experiencing, they got to just enjoy it and be in it. And it was just so easy and fun. It really felt like heaven on Earth during that time... until it wasn't.

N: What was your soul meant to learn from that experience?

V: To experience the beauty. To see the beauty in all things and to let life be easy and to be in flow and to just work when the people are there and to be with them and spend time with them and love them. I never rushed them.

But mainly just to experience the beauty of not only the place where I was living and everything around me, but to be able to experience how good it felt to be able to help people.

N: Yes. Beautiful. Now let's go ahead and drift away from that life, from that scene.

I know the Higher Self could have brought forth many different visions for V to see today. When you first chose to bring her to the cloud area where the people in robes gathered around to greet her, why did you pick that vision to show her today?

V: To let her know how supported she is and how loved she is and how we come to her, always gathering around her, loving her.

N: And who were those people?

V: They were her angels and a man. God!

N: Yes, beautiful! Why was that important for her to see given what's going on in her life now?

V: So she can just be reminded of how supported she is and how surrounded by divine energy she is. There's nothing but total unconditional love for this woman.

N: You also chose to bring forward the vision of her looking at an empty-looking planet. Why did you pick that vision to show her?

V: This is where she's from, this is her land and she did train here. This is her home. And since she has been gone, that land is no more and that's okay, but she so often yearns to go back home… often feeling like she doesn't belong here. But she needed to see that that is no longer an option, and that this is her home, and she needs to be comfortable here.

N: She carries the essence of that life and that place with her here, doesn't she?

V: Yes, it's who she is. It is where she's from. So it will always be a part of her.

N: Would it be helpful for her to know the name of that place? (No.)
    Okay. Is there anything else you want her to know about that life that you showed her?

V: From that galaxy, from that planet, from that area, from that realm... that is where her gifts are from. Her gifts are not of this world at all... the earthly plane. And so for her to be able to remember where she is from and understand the impact that she is here to make and that she really was prepared for this, she trained, she was prepared, she was groomed, she was taught to be able to bring all of these gifts from this planet that she is from... it's important that she understands that it's just not some whim, that this was very well orchestrated.

N: She's right where she's meant to be. (Yes.)
   Does she wonder about that sometimes?

V: She wonders about that all the time. Yes. And she's exactly where she needs to be, doing exactly what she needs to be doing.

N: Yes. And she has all the support she needs. (Yes.)
   What is V's soul mission in this lifetime?

V: To be joy, to spread joy and to do this through helping others release their pain. And through releasing their pain and their stuckness and their density, that will help them get closer to their joy. But she has to be the example. She has to show what it looks like so that others can say, "I want that. I want to feel like that."

So, she has to *be* that joy. She has to share that joy, and as she does that, that's what people will be drawn to. That's how people will know how to find her... is through her joy.

N: Why is this mission so important for V?

V: This mission is so important to V because she knows it's in her DNA. She knows that she's here to help change lives, and she is. She is. And she's done it before, and she knows that, and she remembers that, and she knows that it's possible.

N: So, she's doing a good job with it?

V: Yes. She definitely gets caught up, though, more than she needs to… because if she can remember that her real purpose and mission here is to spread joy, then when you get caught up in all the silly little things, that takes away your joy.

N: It can be a lot more simple than she makes it out to be.

V: Yes. Yes it can.

N: Beautiful. V feels as if there is a part of her wealth that she's not able to access, that maybe she blocks herself from. How can V access more wealth?

V: It's all in her flow. The more she flows with everything that she is experiencing, and the more that she shares her experience, knowing that this is medicine for anyone that needs to hear it and experience it for themselves. It's like V can be the example of what is possible, and she's the one that is the actual example of, "Oh, hey, I'm going through this, so that I can get to this." So, she just needs to be the example and flow. There is no final destination. She just needs to go with the flow.

N: What keeps her from going with the flow?

V: Well, she is always trying to get to that next point, that next place. And the anticipation of trying to get there is keeping her away, because she's thinking of the future. And if she can just be present and take action and share her journey and share what she's learning in that moment, teach what she is learning, then that is when she's in flow.

N: So, being concerned with not receiving the wealth keeps her out of the present moment sometimes?

V: Yeah. She thinks that there is more, and there really is no more. She is receiving what she needs to receive right now, and as she expands and grows, so will her wealth. Ha, there you go.

N: Yes. But she's already on track to.

V: Yes. She's doing so beautifully. We are all so proud of her. We were not expecting any of this, actually, not on this level. She's above and beyond where we thought she would be. Honestly, she has gone above and beyond where we thought she could go and would go in this lifetime. So, she's already broken records. It's fine.

N: The wealth isn't a representation of her growth and expansion or worth. (Yes.)

Wow, that's so beautiful. Thank you. V has been feeling like she's here to create some sort of system around helping others do the work that she does for people. Is that true, that she's here to create a system or a framework for others?

V: Yes. It's like it's a triangle. So, if you can imagine a triangle, and the tip of the triangle is the joy, that's like the peak that everyone wants to get to. And so if we can start at the bottom—or work through the density and the layers of merging the density on that bottom layer—then it's like, as we clear that out, then we get to go higher and we're getting closer and closer and closer up into that joy.

And so at the very bottom of that triangle is this breath that she works with. It really is imperative that you use the breath to help clear out all of this density. So, breath, first and foremost. And then as we move up, that is when we begin to use our voice, because the voice will help clear the frequency within. It will help the chakras vibrate at these certain vibrational tones or frequencies of each energy center in the body. And so the voice is very important. As we're clearing out using the breath, the voice will help, I guess, calibrate. Yes, that's the word. Calibrate the chakra system. And then, as we are becoming more calibrated, then that is when there's more flow in the body. And, as we have more flow in the body, that is when we reach higher levels of ecstasy. And so yes, it's like a little pyramid.

N: So, does she already know everything she needs to know to create the system?

V: Yes. Oh goodness! Yeah, she knows everything.

N: (Chuckles) Why does she feel like there might be something missing sometimes?

V: Because if she actually created this, then it might be successful, and if it's successful, that means she might be successful.

N: Where does this fear of success come from?

V: Hmm, where does this fear of success come from? I feel like they're going back in the Rolodex because there's a lot of layers that have kept her from... that have been very layered on top of each other. So, it's like, I can't remember which one, where it started from, because it's so deep.

The Rolodex is so deep. It's like, well... (makes sounds as if flipping through each layer)... but when I get down to the bottom of it, the Rolodex, there's just this little seed. It just feels like this little knot inside of her little sacral area. This is like that little poke, that little something.

N: How can she heal the fear of success even though it has built up so many layers at this point? What will it take?

V: It's going to take her taking the action steps and trusting that it'll all work out, because it will all work out. It's already done. We've already set everything in motion for her.

N: Yes. So, she doesn't need to worry about success.

V: No, no. Everything is... it's already done.

N: There's no risk in becoming more successful. And what will happen if she allows herself to be more successful?

V: It's like she will be reminded of what is possible, because she's forgotten how good it can be, and we just want her to remember the depth of magic and beauty that is available to her because she knows, but she forgot. It's like she knows the possibilities and the potential and the magic that is available, but because of the layers of the fears, it has created that dissonance between her inner knowing and the outer reality.

N: Now that she knows about this fear, can we help her release it today?

V: That would be nice. We can do that.

N: Okay. Obviously, she will do her part as well, but if we can do anything to make that easier for her, and more pleasant, that'd be amazing.

Note: V has the ability to channel light language, a multidimensional language that brings sound and energy from spirit into the physical world. It can be expressed through the voice through singing, toning, chanting, or speaking, as well as through the use of intuitive hand gestures. It is not something that is meant to be understood by the human mind; it is something you feel deep inside your heart as powerful vibrations and codes are brought through to support in processing shifts in consciousness and the release of deeply held blockages and beliefs that no longer serve us.

V: I'm going to place my hand at the top of this pile of this Rolodex, and just like she channels for her clients, she channels from such a very high dimensional frequency that what she channels breaks down the density. And so we're going to do that now with her because it's high, and so we're just going to channel it for her. (Speaks light language) We're just going to break it down. (More light language)

(Speaking to herself) I know there's some emotion there and it's okay. You can let that go now. You can let it move through you. (Light language) It's okay for you to feel the emotion, V. It's okay. (Light language) Now that we are getting into the nitty gritty of this little seed, we're getting closer down into that memory into the core.

Because this is in your sacral chakra, maybe more of the right side, which is your masculine energy... (deep breath)... which is your energy of action and doing and producing, we can clear this. And because there's been such a disconnection for so long to your masculine energy... (deep breath)... it makes sense that you would have this little block right here.

Let me just do a rundown, make sure this Rolodex is clear, has collapsed and been blown away. Just soften. Okay. Okay. She's good there.

N: Thank you so much. What will she notice differently after today's session?

V: There shouldn't be as much resistance in taking action towards the little things. It's just the little things that could really add up to make things a bigger thing. She just keeps looking at the big thing and it looks too big. And so now she should be able to look at all the tiny little tasks and not feel so overwhelmed with them.

N: Yes. And she'll be able to flow with them more easily too, won't she? (Exactly.)

And feel more joy while she does it, I'm sure, as well. (Yes.)

Beautiful. Since we are talking about V's body, she's wondering how she can best support herself with the aging process. What do you have to share with her about that?

V: She's always been in good shape with great energy, and she's had a lovely... a fine body... and she is getting caught up in the loop of the society standards of aging. She has fallen victim to the propaganda of aging, and so for her to reclaim her inner wisdom and knowledge, she knows exactly what she needs to be doing. She is just not doing it. She knows we tell her what she needs to be doing.

N: Why doesn't she do it?

V: Because she is in the habit of not finishing what she starts. (Laughs) And that's okay. That's okay that she is that way. It is just who she is. She's made it such a bad thing, and it's not a bad thing. It's not that she doesn't finish what she starts - she just doesn't give herself enough credit for what she does start. She starts and finishes plenty, but again, she's just always looking at the big picture and that was overwhelming. Even the body stuff, the supplements that she knows she needs to take instead of just being like, "I've got to take these for the rest of my life," you know, just take them today.

N: Yes. Break things down into smaller steps and focus on the experience in the present. (Yes.)

So, she already knows what she needs to do, and you will assist in continuing to remind her?

V: Yes. Yes. And hopefully now that we've cleared out some of that

Rolodex of blockage, that heaviness that was weighing on her right there, she'll feel a little more light in her feet to go take action.

N: Yes, exactly. She can be successful in all ways, including the aging process and being at peace and empowered with it.

V would love to have a better understanding of her channeling work. Any dimensions, any names, any frequencies, anything like that, that might assist her or just pique her curiosity?

V: Well, just as we were able to facilitate this healing with her, we just channel what is needed. That is all she does. She just channels what is needed. It doesn't matter where it's coming from. There's no name. It's just the frequencies that she works with.

N: What about this connection with the Divine Mother that has been brought to her attention lately? What would you like her to know about that?

V: [V] is a divine being and she is a channel for the Divine Mother of unconditional love. And she had to first be willing to receive that for herself before she could pour that level of unconditional love into anyone else. And she truly has this for herself now. She really does have unconditional love for herself, and so, because she has cultivated that within herself now, she is really able to pour that into other people.

And so that is a part of her gift, and this is the part where we really were not expecting her gifts to expand to this level. She went above and beyond. And because she did, what she has allowed in is the thing that has expanded her gifts on such a deeper level, and so it will continue to unfold. It will continue to become greater than she could imagine because she definitely has never worked in these realms before, even in prior lifetimes. This is all very, very new to her. And so there's a learning curve here, but because she already exists within this unconditional love, it will be very easy for her to navigate through this learning. This unconditional love is just incorporated in all that she does. It already is. It is who she is. She is unconditional love. She truly is.

N: Yes. What was the catalyst that allowed her to go above and beyond? Was there anything in particular that she did or embraced to allow this shift to happen for herself?

V: It was that desire in her heart that she just kept following, and it really did put her on a fast track of very fast, speedy healing. Like she was on a mission! And she just kept going, and it just went above and beyond.

N: Beautiful. How does her work with masculine and feminine energy correlate with the energies of the Divine Mother and Father?

V: Well, it's all connected. It's all connected, because there is the Divine Mother and there is the Divine Father, but it is all one within each other. It's like one big circle of love. And the more that you can allow that feminine and masculine energy to circle with each other, to combine together so that it is becoming one with each other in this circle of love, the more that it is connected. (Draws a circle in the air)

And it's like it's coming together, coming together, coming together. It's like the circle gets faster and faster, faster, and it's like boom, right there at that spot right there where it all comes together as one. That is the oneness, that is the masculine and feminine energies, that is the holiest of holy coming together as one.

It is the Creator, but there are the aspects… the feminine and masculine aspects. So, really, when she's channeling the Divine Mother, she's channeling God—the feminine aspect of God—because that is what the world needs right now. And so that is what is moving through her, so that she can share that, because that's what she does. She channels whatever is needed.

N: Yes. Beautiful. Lately, she's been receiving messages and impressions from Gaia. What is that all about?

V: That is about the surge of energy that is rising from Mother Earth. It is a horrific situation... what is happening to Gaia. And her energy is rumbling. She's becoming angry. Angry because she's been mistreated for so long.

And isn't it funny... right? She is the feminine energy, just like the feminine energies that have been suppressed for all these years. And so, as she is rising, we are rising. And that anger that she feels, that is stirring within her, that is the energy that V is feeling that is rising up through her feet. That is the anger. It is the passion, it is the fuel, it is the fire, and it is imperative that we allow her to breathe.

It is imperative that we allow Mother Earth to breathe, and the way that she can breathe is through us. We are the vessel of breath for her. The more that we breathe, the more that we allow that breath to move through us, the more we are an expression of her. And that's how we will heal this world. This is how we will heal her is through our own breath... is through our own expression of her moving through us... to feel the anger, to feel the passion.

We have to feel it. We have to. She is our fuel, she is our fire, she is our everything that is of this earthly experience. We're here on this land with her. And so, as she is rising, as she is expanding, it is done through us. And so we must honor her. We must listen to her. We must let her energy move through our feet so that we can heal this world.

N: Beautiful. And so, is V working with Gaia in the best way or how would you like her to further work with this energy and expand it out to incorporate it with what she does with other people?

V: This is where V can talk louder. V needs to be talking about this. She needs to be talking about the energy that is pulsing through Mother

Earth and how her feminine energy has been suffocated and suppressed. And she can't take it anymore, just like every other woman.

But every other woman has experienced that because she (Mother Earth) experienced it first. So, because she can't take it anymore, she's rising and her energy is making everyone else rise. And so, it takes a voice. It takes a bold, brave voice to speak of these things and to teach people how to connect to the energies of Gaia, and to teach people to be so bold and brave as to receive that energy and those frequencies themselves.

So, she needs to be talking more about what is happening with the feminine energy, and more about how it has been suppressed, and how connected it is to Earth, that it did happen to her (Gaia) first. It's like her energy was constricted, pulled, and the same thing happened to each one of us. And so now as it is expanding again, it's all happening within each one of us.

So, there was a constriction, and now we're in the middle of an expansion, because all things must constrict to expand. And so, we are in the middle of a great expansion—of a great revolution of expansion—of reclaiming the divine feminine energy. And because V is so connected to this unconditional love, and she is so connected to the Divine Mother aspects of the cosmos, she is able to be a vessel to bring it back down into this earthly plane. Yep, there you go.

N: Yes. Amazing. And she'll continue to allow that to move through her, won't she?

V: Yes. Especially now that she understands the connection between the Divine Mother and her channel from the cosmos. This makes sense. This connects it for her to understand that she's working with the Divine Mother of the Cosmos and the Divine Feminine of Mother Earth. And as we can pull these two frequencies together, that's where it's like we're pulling it in like this... (Makes a hand gesture of pulling something in)

N: And as within, so without. As above, so below. (Exactly.)

That's beautiful. So, she's working on many levels... like personal, collective, and beyond. (Yes. Yes.)

I love it. I'd like to talk more about some of the issues that V has been experiencing in her body now. She's been having some issues with her vision, and I'm curious what has been causing this.

V: Yes, I'm aware she's been praying for a miracle and I'm not sure that we can do that, but we can try. Should we try?

N: I know you can do it.

V: We can try. We can try. I just need to get V on board with this because we told her, "You can't ask for a miracle and then wonder if it's going to happen." (Both chuckle) Alright, let's see what we can do here...

I am pouring frequencies of high dimensional healing into her, and she saw green, which was her heart [chakra] pouring into her eyes. And then now it is just a big white light that she's seeing, and I'm just penetrating in through the back of her eyes. Just rubbing all of the eyes. They've been so itchy lately. (Rubs her eyes)

She's been rubbing them and it feels so good, but we just need to go a little bit deeper. It's like she was already preparing for this, but she just couldn't get in deep enough.

N: Would it be useful for her to know where these issues originated from?

V: Well, it's interesting, because she had this little rash around her eyes on her skin recently and we told her that she needed to see things from just a different perspective. She was just getting a little stuck in her own stuff, and so this rash started forming around her eyes, both of them. And so we just put that there so she would start moving her eyes around, so she would rub her eyes more.

So, this is really what she needs to be doing is just moving her eyes a little bit more, because it feels so good to her and it's really getting deeper into all of the thickness that's pulling her eyes back. And it's like the more she can just move that and get the blood flowing back through these muscles, then it will really help her vision, and it will help her wrinkles so she doesn't feel like she looks so old.

N: You mentioned wanting her to see things from a different perspective. How would you like her to do that?

V: Well, she was just getting very caught up again in the "how" and the "what" and all of that stuff, and we just wanted her to see that she just needed to stop looking at it that way. And she knew as soon as she got the little outbreak on her eye, she knew it was a sign of being able to see things differently, but she hasn't been doing it yet.

We can give her the message and the sign, but that doesn't mean that she's going to change everything. But she's doing better. Because all this stuff is starting to back up within her now, it is forcing her to see it again. So, now that it's up, she's seeing it, she's working through it again, and that's good.

N: So, was she putting her blinders on around something that was important?

V: Yeah, she was putting the blinders on... just looking at it like, "This is the way to do things, the way that I have to move forward," instead of just soaking up everything that was available to her. Just like the beauty and the joy and the magic that was all around her.

N: Yes. So, now that she knows this, and now that she's had more healing with her eyes, what will she notice after the session with her eyes?

V: Things should seem a lot brighter, a lot more clear for her, and she needs to keep moving her eyes around and allowing her fingertips to go in there and to work on the muscles behind her eyes. I know that sounds like it might be impossible, but she can do it. It's like the way that she will know how to move her hands will really help get the blood flow back through those deeper muscles that are behind her eyes.

N: Can you also help her with this healing tonight in her sleep?

V: Yes. I'll continue to work with her on this because I know it does mean a lot to her, so I'll continue to do that.

N: Amazing. V has also been concerned about gaining a little bit extra weight than she's used to lately. What is this originating from?

V: Well, she's in this holding pattern lately of holding onto things... onto her past, onto her old habits, onto her old beliefs, onto all the old stuff. She's still hanging onto all this old stuff, and so as she begins to let go and take action on these intuitive little nudges that are moving through her... as she begins to move and to let go, so will some of this.

And then going back to that healing with the clearing out the Rolodex, helping to move out some of that will help her to take those action steps better and faster. So, it's all connected. It's like she'll start taking those little action steps and then automatically she'll start to let go. Because she'll be letting go [of the past], she'll be doing things, she'll be taking action and she'll be moving, and that will all help alleviate some of that little weight she's been holding on to.

N: So, whenever she notices the extra weight, it's a reminder to her that she's holding on to things that she doesn't need to carry any longer?

V: Yes. That's perfect.

N: Okay, amazing. Can we do any healing for her right now to help her let go a little bit more easily?

V: Yes! I would love to do a little full body scan on her and just kind of clear out whatever is in the way. We're already moving some energy in her ankles right now, helping her to move without the density of concrete feet, putting a little pep in her step, shall we say.

And then also with this ankle and leg stuff, it will help her connect more to Gaia to receive more of her messages because all of that energy moves through your feet. So, when we always encourage people to go get grounded and go stand barefoot out into Mother Earth it really… it is really true. So, clearing out these ankles…

It's rather dense in there, and so we're just having to clear out a lot, especially on this left side, shaking it out, and it's moving up through her knees and through her thighs, her glute area, which is connected to her lower back.

N: And what's going on with the lower back?

V: Well, that is where she's holding onto the past, and all that pain is connected to what you're holding onto in the past. So, just some of those old habits, some of those old ways of being that she's still attached to. We can let some of that go and clear out that attachment. There we go.

Now we're moving up to the front of her stomach area, being sure to cross back over that area where that little seed, little stone, little nastiness [from the fear of success that] was in there… moving up through the rib cage, chest, through that beautiful heart, her arms, her throat chakra, moving up around the ears, face, the front of the face, the back of the head, pulling it right off the top of her head, releasing it.

N: What effects will this have on V moving forward?

V: She's been eating sugars and things that have settled in her joints, and she's been feeling a little achy and tired lately, so this should be able to move through her. [It will encourage] her wanting to make better decisions and thinking about what she puts in her body, how it's going to ultimately affect her. So, hopefully, this has cleared out some of the joint density, and we can take it easy on the sugar, and it shouldn't be a problem.

N: Wonderful. Before we go, are there any last messages you'd like to share with V today?

V: Yes. I just want to say that we love you so, so, so much and we are so proud of you and really, truly your only job and purpose currently is to have fun in all that you do. Try to bring that joy, just have fun. Don't think too far in the future.

And be really proud of yourself because we are so proud of you. So, you need to be really proud of yourself because you have done above and beyond what we were excited for you to experience. So, celebrate yourself, love yourself, and just know that we are really working out everything for you. All you have to do is take action on the intuitive nudges that you receive. That is all you have to do, everything else is already being done.

N: Beautiful. Are you complete? (Yes.)
Amazing. Thank you very, very much.

V: Thank you, thank you, thank you.

Chapter 10: Merging with Your Higher Self

It is my belief that we are here to eventually learn to merge more fully with our Higher Selves. Becoming our fully healed selves means becoming more integrated with the "wholeness" that is our Higher Self. This reintegration happens when we combine what we have learned from all our lifetimes and embody the highest expression of those energies within one soul. Only then can we transcend this physical world and become Ascended Masters ourselves.

While it is a common reminder in spiritual circles for us to "live in the moment" and "be here now," revisiting our past and parallel lives can be a helpful way for us to tie together all the loose energetic threads we have not yet fully integrated. When we do this, we can live more fully anchored in our expanded awareness in the present moment without being rooted in the fear and other unhealthy compulsions we picked up in the past. The word "past" may not even be the best way to describe when these other expressions of our soul occurred, especially if their influence still affects who we are and how we operate in the present moment.

Since my first hypnosis session, which was featured at the beginning of this book, I've had the opportunity to receive multiple sessions from various other practitioners. Each hypnosis practitioner has their own style and specific area of expertise. Different practitioners bring out different experiences for the client, just like how each client provides a completely different journey for the practitioner to witness. This is because the conversation is always led through the frame of reference of both the client and the person guiding the session. The studies and natural abilities of the hypnosis practitioner will widen their frame of reference, making it possible for them to create a healing container for different levels of information that may want to come through.

Bridget Renee Holliday, the hypnosis practitioner I worked with for the session you'll read next, has a special interest in working with galactic energies. She has been aware of her psychic abilities since birth and was able to channel information while making healing suggestions as she guided the session.

My goal for this next-level session, which occurred approximately one year after my first session, was to learn more about the more cosmically inclined aspect of myself. I wanted to know whether I had significant past or parallel lives on other planets. I wanted to understand the nature of the Higher Self. And I also wanted to understand some of the messages my Higher Self seemed to be trying to get through to me through the intuitive messages I had been receiving over the span of many months.

One message that constantly came through in my meditations or whenever I asked for intuitive guidance from my Higher Self was the phrase *"Color me wonderful."* It seemed to always be repeating in my head. I spent a great deal of time searching for the meaning of this phrase to no avail. I knew I needed to ask the Higher Self directly if I was going to get clarity. What I discovered was not only the secret hidden meaning of this phrase that had been planted in my subconscious by my Higher Self but a more vibrant, visceral understanding of what it meant to merge with the Higher Self itself.

At the time of this session, I had just completed my hypnosis training but had yet to conduct any sessions for others. I was struggling to decide how I would describe this healing practice I was going to be facilitating. I worried that others would think it was too weird or "out there" to want to work with me. I had studied to become an Angel Messenger in the past—which is an energy most people equate with love and light—but how would I explain the energies I was working with now? With quantum hypnosis, there is a revelation of both darkness and light, which can be uncomfortable for some to witness.

In the session I am sharing in this final chapter, I was allowed to experience myself as my Higher Self so I could explain what it feels like to see things from their higher perspective. I could feel and sense how my Higher Self viewed *me*, as its earthly human counterpart, and how the energy on that higher level is connected to the bigger picture of the whole universe. I was able to feel the love and trust that emanated from this larger energetic aspect of myself so that I could feel calm and safe working with it and trust all of the messages that came through me, as well as through my clients.

Through this expanded awareness of my Higher Self, I could also zoom out and experience an interesting phenomenon of operating on multiple dimensions at the same time. There was my Higher Self and my human self, but there are also many other layers and levels concurrently at play in between, including galactic energies from other worlds and planets that I am embodying simultaneously. This may be very difficult to understand to our human selves as it is truly the next level of spiritual evolutionary advancement. As usual, the more you think you know about the Higher Self, the more you will realize how little you really know.

B: I want you to tell me now... are you inside, outside, or in space?

N: Inside.

B: Beautiful. And as you are inside, what does it look like where you are?

N: It's my old bedroom (in my present lifetime).

B: Beautiful. And as you are inside your old bedroom, what is happening in this moment?

N: I could tell it's my old bedroom because the first thing I saw was a hanger. I hung my clothes backward in that closet because of the way it was shaped. So, that was the first thing I saw, and then my rug that I had in that room. And it's all set up just the way I had it.

B: And how does it feel to be back in your old bedroom?

N: I feel like they're showing me, oh... (Starts crying) They're bringing me to an experience that I had there. I don't know why I'm crying. It was a good experience.

B: Okay, just let the feelings flow. It's fine. I'm holding space with you.

N: (Crying) This is something I was wondering about but I didn't ask about.

B: Beautiful. So, what are they showing you?

N: I was studying to be an Angel Messenger. I had a really big awakening, and I spent eight days just completely downloading intuitive insights constantly, 24/7, all day, all night. (Deep sigh)

I had an air purifier in my room and it sounded like angel music. Normally, it just sounded normal, but that week it sounded like angels singing.

At the end of that week, I took a bath. I was laying in the bathtub, and I looked down at my feet, and I realized that I was an alien for the first time and I was, like, shocked! (Both laugh) I was new to this whole thing, so I was horrified... but I knew at the same time, so I didn't know what to think.

I always painted my toenails blue, and I realized that blue was all over my whole life. My sheets, my walls, my chair, my phone… it was the same shade of blue everywhere. Sometimes I couldn't even find my phone because it matched everything in my whole house.

B: And were you blue as your star being?

N: Must have been because it's everywhere all the time. My pots and pans are blue. Everything's the same shade of blue. This pillow I'm on. (Sighs)

I just didn't know what was happening to me that week because I was taking these angel classes, and it was like we don't actually learn anything in the class. [The teacher] just talks, and it's like, "How am I supposed to be an angel messenger from this class? We're not even doing anything." (Laughs)

But then I realized [the messenger training] was all happening just in my reality, and that the angels were teaching me. I've had spiritual awakenings before, but this one was like, "Whoa."

B: That's beautiful. Can we ask the angelics and your Higher Self to explain the blue? Ask your Higher Self to bring in the wisdom and the knowingness of how the blue is connected to this… what I imagine is an aspect of you, yes? Is this a parallel or simultaneous life you are living? Are you what we call a galactic being?

N: It's a safe, calming color for me, because it reminds me of my environment… it's like seeping into this reality. It brings me calm. It's the vibration of the color. It reminds me of who I am.

B: And who are you?

N: Pleiadian. (Crying)

After I looked down and I saw my toenails were blue, and I realized I had been painting them blue for like five years, I got scared and I started painting them pink ever since. (Laughs)

B: Can we release that fear now? Are you ready to release it?

N: (Deep sigh) Yeah. I'm not afraid. It's okay to like pink, too.

B: Of course it is, of course it is.

N: I'm just so grateful... (Bursts out crying more)... that they're bringing me here.

B: What are you feeling and seeing now?

N: This is an experience I need to... I just need to come back to it and heal, just integrate, and I'm just really grateful. (Deep sigh)

After that experience, I started filling my world with pink and turquoise. I remember, one weekend, I bought a bunch of clothes online and I didn't even think about it. When they arrived, they were all pink, and I didn't even realize. All these packages started arriving. They just started coming... Because things take forever to arrive in Hawaii, I just completely forgot. Day after day, I would go to my front door and there's pink leggings and a pink dress and pink everything. (Both laughing)

B: Oh my gosh.

N: It's two sides of me I'm bringing together. I think it's like I'm a hybrid and one side is Pleiadian and one side is Arcturian, and I'm learning to be both, access both simultaneously. Part of it is like a healing between the two... I don't know... races?

B: Like they're coming together in unity?

N: Yeah, it's like it's healing for them to experience it through me. Or "them" could be *me* even, I don't know!

B: Mmm, I love that. Turquoise, teal and aqua are my favorite colors and they're everywhere.

N: I noticed. I've been noticing my starseed friends love those colors, too, and I've been very curious about that because I'll meet them and they're like-minded souls and they love the same colors.

I'm just thinking about how blue and pink make purple. One of my friends came to visit me, and she brought me a purple pillowcase, and now I have purple starting to slowly seep in. And lavender, I love lavender. The smell. It is symbolic of the union, not separation.

B: Yes. Unity. Can we ask the Higher Self to show you through feeling and being, and visually as well, what your Pleiadian/Arcturian connection is, so that we can fully integrate and anchor those frequencies into Natalie's human expression here on Earth in a way that is highly beneficial, highly supportive, uplifting and of service? And just describe what is happening.

N: I'm part of the joint council between them. This is what "color me wonderful" is. (Sobbing)

B: Love it.

N: I wanted to be embodied as both [galactic races] in the human form.
I don't know why I'm crying about it! (Crying and laughing)

B: Okay. Do you miss it? Have you been missing it or does it feel good?

N: (Still crying) I'm excited. I'm excited about this life. I often think about how much I love this life, and people say, "Oh, it's so hard," or whatever, and I'm like, "I love it!" (Laughing)

I'm excited about this experiment as an adventure of fusing different forces together that the world needs in an embodied state.

And really, I am not either [side]. I'm both, but it's more than that. It's like how we have a personality on Earth, but even this level of being part of both galactic councils is an offshoot of something even greater. It's like a layer within a layer. It's a projection, too.

B: Totally. And we're connected and communicating with all of them, yes? Are you feeling that?

N: Yeah. When I had that angelic awakening, I felt like a funnel had cracked open in my crown chakra, and I started to hear the angels more strongly. I was thinking, "This is so normal," but time has gone on—it's been two years since then—and I just have felt very human. I just don't have such visceral experiences anymore because I'm... I'm anchoring it, embodying it in more of a three-dimensional state. I think sometimes I feel abandoned or something. (Crying) The intuitive connection is so strong sometimes, and then it's just not.

B: Can we clear the feelings of abandonment? Let's do that now. Asking Higher Self—hello, beautiful Higher Self—and the angelics and our beautiful galactic family and any other beautiful high frequency beings connected with Natalie. Asking for assistance and clearing the feeling and the programming of being abandoned, and instead bringing in and expanding into a deep awareness of how divinely connected Natalie is to herself, to Higher Self, to soul team collective, to her Pleiadian and Arcturian aspects, and to anyone within our collective, including our beautiful planet and our co-inhabitants!

Let's go ahead and transmute or reprogram, whatever is appropriate, anything connected to separation consciousness, and the illusion of separation, and the veils of forgetting that are appropriate to do so now. Let the wisdom, guidance, knowledge, codes, keys, frequencies of her soul, Higher Self, and soul team collective... let it be loud, clear, and obvious in all now moments going forward from this one, deeply tuned in and in a very seamless streamlined, harmonious and balanced way that is fully integrated and anchored so that Natalie may always be connected to her expansiveness in a very conscious way while at the same time experiencing the groundedness that she is embodying as well.

And how does this feel?

N: Like a fusion and a healing balm.

I know I knew this on a higher level, but it's like when... I don't want to say when I'm not as connected... but when I wasn't fully in fusion [with the higher realms], it was like I'm mining. I'm digging down into the three-dimensional to infuse the energy there, and it's just all part of the project.

I don't even think I felt truly sad about the disconnection, but I was aware that I was feeling like I was kind of in a humdrum, monotonous experience in 3D, and now it's just about fusing the joint visions together.

It's like how a bug has lots of different eyes and it's just coming together into one... like... nucleus almost. Because, really, my job here is to dig deep down into the physical Earth and bring these higher frequencies here. So, I did have to go through that experience—of the cutting off of intuitive abilities—but I don't have to anymore.

B: You can anchor them in just by being a conduit of whatever is appropriate, yes?

N: And consciously, co-creatingly. The work I'm doing—most people around me have never heard of QHHT®—and I feel this desire to explain it in my own way that bridges it for them. Whereas people have heard of astrology, they haven't often heard of this, and I feel this natural desire to translate it in a way that's welcoming... welcoming them up the stairway, and myself as well, through *them* experiencing it.

I'm just so excited about it. I'm excited to bring the three-dimensional friends into the four-dimensional and higher worlds. I just see myself standing at the bottom of a staircase holding my hand out.

And I'm seeing another place where I used to live, a house that I renovated while I was living in it many years ago. It's where I learned about angels being real for the first time, and I had this remembrance. I was literally just walking down the stairs, and I was at the bottom of the stairs, and I remembered that... (Sighs) I remembered that I was an angel. So many of us are, and we all knew we were in on the secret.

I literally had just seen a woman (Lorna Byrne) who could see angels on a video. Her book was called *Angels in My Hair*. The next morning, I woke up, and I looked in the mirror, and I had a feather in my hair.

I feel like that's coming in because the pink color is also a safe haven for me with the angels. It's like heart energy, heart chakra...

B: ...Soft, fluffy, bunny, heart energy! That's what I like to think about pink.

N: I feel like it has just reminded me of that heritage almost, too. That's one of the energies that's merging with the blue and the pink and the purple. Like the Arcturian, Pleiadian, and Angelic [soul properties] are all friends. I just see a dropper and it's like a drip-dropping of colors into a little Petri dish. And it's like, that's me! That's who I am! I'm all these energies. And it's really important for me to merge them at this time because I had an awareness of them that they are separate areas of myself. (Deep breath)

B: Can we assist with that to merge even more today for all three of them? (Yeah.)

Let's just bring them into the full wholeness that they are, allowing the beautiful frequencies that Natalie is. We'll specifically focus on the Arcturian, Pleiadian, Angelic frequencies and merging them in ways that are beautiful, so aligned, congruent, and harmonious, and any other of the frequencies that are appropriate at this time to merge into this as well for Natalie, let's go ahead and do that as well.

We can bring it in, allowing Natalie to always have access to her high knowingness for any of her questions, for her deep remembrances of who she is on a soul level and all of the simultaneous expressions of her soul as appropriate and in the highest good. Bringing that in, in ways that feel aligned and gentle… in ways that are easy and effortless, so that she can remember who she is deeply and why she is here.

What are we experiencing right now?

N: (Sniffles) So many things. (Laughs) So many things.

Archangel Gabriel and Haniel came in. That makes a lot of sense. It's like "communicating" the "intuitive knowing".

Note: Gabriel is known as the Archangel with the power to communicate God's will to humanity. Haniel is the Archangel of intuitive guidance.

N: I just saw mixing more colors. They're reminding me that I love the color white.

B: Me too.

N: I'm just thinking of where I live. It's all these colors! I love white furniture. And so, they added white—white light energy—and it started to turn this luminescent purple, like the inside of an abalone shell that you put sage in. And that's a color I love so much when I think of the higher realms. It's like this sparkly white with a rainbow inside…

B: Prismatic?

N: Yes. So, they added that to the mix and I just kept feeling like I'm so grateful to have the integration [of all these energies].

I am looking down at me, my presence, and I just see myself. I just love myself from this higher perspective that's beyond Natalie. And I just feel so precious about her. (Crying deeply)

I just love her so much. I'm grieving when she feels the sadness and darkness that all humans feel. It's not specific to her, but I feel that flowing out through this process and just cracking open these higher layers. They're uniting, like how an onion has the different layers. You peel off the outer layer before you cut it. There's no division. It's all melting into this onion soup. (Both laugh)

It's just really funny because last night I made a sauce where I cut up this onion and I blended it into a sauce, and I thought, "This is the weirdest thing I've ever made." It was a new recipe. And when I finally finished it and I ate it, all I could taste was onions, even though I put so many other things in it.

So yeah, it's just a good integration of this whole energetic sphere. It's like I'm a marble with all the different colors in it. I'm just seeing all the connections.

I was just really touched by the perspective of seeing myself almost as... I don't want to say a "pet" because that's kind of demeaning... but I don't have the word to describe it.

B: From that aspect of our expanded consciousness, that aspect of our soul, we love the human part of us like it's our child. It's those people like us that love our animals fully and completely, super unconditionally, deeply, beautifully. Almost like maternal and paternal, mixed together. Love from a healthy standpoint. Is that what it's like?

N: It's kind of like being my own angel. (Yes.)

And I'm experiencing the love. It's just endless. It's just so deep and vast like that white, luminous, luminescent, slightly purple, slightly green, slightly every color!

And it's interesting because, for the past year, if I get a reading or Reiki, I'm told, "You need to paint. You have to mix colors, you have to mix colors." In my first hypnosis session, all my ancestors came in. I didn't even know that could happen. And they're all like, "You have to paint. You have to paint!"

So, for the last year I've been painting, thinking, "Oh, I'm going to do something with this"... that human level [thinking]. But they just kept saying, "It's not for any purpose. It's not for what you think." And now I'm just realizing, okay, I get it. I'm getting it. It's representative of the fusing of the colors and energies within me.

B: Is it bringing it into the physical as well? Is it anchoring it?

N: Yeah. I need to be this expanded version of myself now. For the new phase I'm moving into, it's appropriate for it to be fused. And it's interesting because when I first started painting, I painted with acrylic. But I was frustrated that the mixing wasn't satisfying. So, then I started painting with watercolor, and I just started seeing watercolors in my mind. I didn't even need to paint anymore. I think and dream in watercolor. And it's just all coming home to this experience now, preparing me for it.

I am just so grateful because I studied angel communication, and I was really frustrated with it because I wanted nothing more than to communicate with angels all day. And it just wasn't coming to me anymore. It seemed like it stopped flowing for a while. So, I just feel so much gratitude for just witnessing this coming together.

B: And now going forward from this, Natalie can access her angelic sides, any of the sides that are appropriate and highly beneficial, but also the communication and connection with any of the other soul team collective frequencies. It gets to be easy and effortless. Yes, let's pull that in. Easy, effortless, loud, clear and obvious. Gentle, beautifully uplifting.

Let's ask Higher Self if we're able to lift the illusions of forgetting more palpably for Natalie, bringing in that high divine knowingness, the discernment, turning the volume up on the soul senses, gently, fully integrated, anchored, always balanced, and harmonized.

N: I am a bigger entity. I'm experiencing... it's weird to say "I". We're experiencing ourself as a fully integrated higher entity.

I have these dreams sometimes where I'm planning my life, but I feel like I'm only one of the beings that is a part of that process. It's like I'm on a playground, and [the other spirits will] come pick me up, and they're like, "Okay, it's time to go plan this." I experience myself as this childlike self, and I feel like I'm blocked off from the committee, kind of. There's a whole committee planning my life and I'm just this little child that's part of it. But I feel like that aspect of me is now opening up. I almost see myself growing older, more mature.

B: I love it. That's beautiful.

N: It's interesting. It's like a fractal. I'm me, but I'm all of the [energies I've been], and I can flit in between both.

B: Yeah. It's like a soul stream that is shared amongst all of [our lives]. We are all of them, and we can connect and communicate with all of them that are appropriate for where we are now. Right? (Yeah.)

My first session, my feline Lyran parallel expression simultaneous life came in and showed me that we can connect and communicate with any of the other expressions of our soul, and that it's easy to do when we are embodying our fifth-dimensional and above frequencies, which is what we are moving into more and more on Earth. So, I've been communicating with them since then and many more have come in.

So, can we give this to Natalie as well? Where can we ask the simultaneous lives to come in and show her how easy it is to connect and communicate amongst ourselves so that there is that knowingness and the knowledge and wisdom, but also the connection?

N: They're showing me that when I pick up on these memories of planning my life... that *all* of the people on the planning committee are me.

And this higher entity that I have been bringing together now... all the colors... that's what it is. It's my Higher Self, but not as what I would imagine a Higher Self is previously. It's just a big blob of energies, basically. (Laughs)

B: Like consciousness, energy. And these are the expressions.

N: Yeah. It's not like I'm my big sister (as my Higher Self) and I'm like, "You have to do this" (to my human self). It's so much greater than that. This is what I wanted to explore with QHHT® is the Higher Self and what it is and accessing it. So, that's what I'm experiencing now.

B: Yes, and maybe you can tell me... I have my own knowingness about this, but do you experience yourself as the Higher Self within all the expressions of your soul, within this universal experience and others?

Let's allow Natalie's consciousness to expand a bit, allowing her to have access to this expansive understanding and gently, gently - it's almost like when they stretch shoes so that they can fit someone's feet, right? We are just going to allow it to gently open a bit more... little bits at a time... still anchored in her human, but allowing that anchoring to actually allow Natalie to expand even further, even higher. And really to access and understand that high knowingness in a very conscious way, in a way that is really balanced and harmonized and completely congruent.

So, looking at the Higher Self, these are some questions that Natalie, I'm sure, will have. I had them. I find the Higher Self to be amazing. Are you experiencing that Higher Self is the oneness, but also Higher Self is the dreamer of all the expressions, all the lives? Do you see it as the aspect of us that is essentially the planner, the dreamer, the orchestrator, so to speak... not in a weird controlling way... but in a beautiful divine source expressing kind of way? Is that what you're experiencing now?

N: Yeah. It's so playful and creative.

It just reminds me of when I had my... I don't know if it was... it obviously was not *just* an angelic awakening. (Laughs) Those eight days [when I was downloading universal information], I kept asking, "Why?" Why is the world like this? Why is the universe like that? Every time I'd ask, "Why?", the angels would be like, "Okay, you want to know?" Then they let me know why, and then I'd be like, "But why?" And I just kept going and going and going and going.

And that's how I see the Higher Self. It's a spark of God's source, universal energy. I just feel like there's no boundaries. It just permeates. It's almost like this group of energies—I can't even say "broke off" because that's not even an accurate statement—but they're like, "Hey, let's play with these colors... kind of. Let's see what kind of experiences we can create with these energies." And within each color, there's so many shades. If you look under a microscope of that color, there's so many more expressions of the color than what you can just see from the outside. So yeah, I don't have the words, but I'm experiencing it.

B: I feel like it is... I'll use some of your words and add some... they are a spark of divine source continuing to express in infinite ways that feel aligned and are exciting and joyful in all the things, right? Beautiful source expression, experiences, and experiments, right? (Yeah.)

And all the variations.

N: Yeah, it's fun. That's how I feel. It's just all for fun.

B: To express just because.

Can we ask Natalie's questions?

N: Sure.

B: Beautiful. (Reading her notes) "Question 1: I know I'm a starseed, but why and how did I originally come to Earth?" What else can you tell us about this?

N: It's fun. It's so much fun. It's the ultimate experiment, adventure, opportunity. It's just all for fun. (Deep sigh)

Just have fun. It is not work. It's fun. Stop working. It's not work. It's fun. (Crying)

It's so heavy when you think it's work. It's caught up with fear and conditioning. It's not work. This isn't work. This isn't a job. This isn't a career. This isn't work. It's not for money, it's not for sustenance. It's none of those things. It's a delusion. Break it open, let it go. It's causing you so much pain. Let it go. (Pleading)

B: Can we break the illusion now or dissolve it?

N: Let it go!

B: Let's bring that in. Let's bring that in for Natalie and anyone else on Earth that is ready for this now. Whatever Earth they're on, let's lift the illusions.

N: It's so beautiful. I've been teaching people about doing what they love through their career. It's just so hilarious.

B: That helps them lift the illusion, right?

N: Yeah. This is the next thing they need to know.

B: There are lots of people who are stuck in scarcity and poverty consciousness, and this what Natalie teaches them and helps them illuminate out of those really dense frequencies to be able to explore, and have fun, and enjoy life in a different way than they had ever experienced before.

So, let's honor what Natalie does in that way for people, aligning them with their heart's desires in a world that still values money, and everything revolves around it. So, it's like setting them free from the denser parts of the illusion, yes? So that they can be available for even less dense parts of this experience. So it's a pathway up for people.

N: Yes. I see myself pouring concrete to create concrete steps. And it's like how Natalie feels on the Earth plane, having consciousness channeling through her, and yet she's in a dense field.

I just feel… "condensed" is the word I'm going to use, and I just feel like I long to be free and my full holistic self. I feel like I have to mine down into the Earth and I'm very tired of it, but it's necessary because I'm building a bridge so that I can take my community with me to my next level. You know? Not everyone will come. That's okay. But I'm creating a pathway so that they can come.

For those who are in the more dense frequencies, it has been necessary to teach in this way because astrology has been a bridge. People know astrology, but they don't know QHHT® commonly. And I'm still teaching the same thing - about energy - but the stairwell is getting taller.

B: And wider?

N: Yeah. And this is only temporary. This pouring of the concrete. I'm just integrating more fully into my joy and that aspect of fun. But until I get there, I've just been feeling like it is work and it's dense. But this is helping me connect. That's part of the fun.

I'm just starting to really understand this idea of moving down into density. It's funny, we normally think of it as moving from density to the higher levels, but that's not really what's happening. It's actually the higher going dense to learn! It's so funny.

B: And we're a conduit of knowledge and wisdom, and experience, and all of it is happening back and forth between Gaia and our highest. We're just like a radio tower that's always sending out signals of what we're experiencing because we're all in oneness, right?

N: Yeah. We're pouring this concrete of crystals... and I can never think of the word. It's, like, very hip... tetra... "terrazzo".

B: Terrazzo! Where they have the stones in the floor...

N: And there's shiny pieces and stuff.

B: Usually it's glass, right? But I think it would be awesome if it was crystal.

N: Yeah. It's what we're doing.

B: Oh yeah, we are! We're making the terrazzo.

N: I'm seeing that luminescent white. I wish I could find a better word to describe it... pearlescent. It's moving through me. And this is part of the vast awakening. They're saying "color me wonderful" is all aspects of your Higher Self coming together.

B: Beautiful. I have a question for Natalie's Higher Self. Are you currently experiencing yourself as the Pleiadian, the Arcturian, and the Angelic? Are they three source expressions that you're experiencing yourself as simultaneously right now? And is Natalie a sort of fractal of them as well?

N: Yes, but we don't even like that word "fractal." There's so much love poured into the vessel.

B: We'll just speak as if it is just the three of you and that it might be more. Did the three of you hold the intention to collaborate in this way through the expression of Natalie?

N: Yeah. It's like there were beings of all areas. This is very old energy though. This merging happened long ago. It's not new. It's very ancient. I almost have to dive really deep. It's like there were aspects of those frequencies that were vibrating at a similar level to where they just connected. I see a pinwheel and each [fan] has combined, and has been operating as one for just eons, I want to say. The experiment is in degrading it in the density.

This energy [that is Natalie's Higher Self] has just been flying around doing all sorts of things. That's the fun of this. It's like, "Let's integrate it in the physical reality!" We've been flying around in the ethers this whole time. *This* is what's exciting. This is the leading edge down *here*.

B: That's amazing. Thank you, first of all, for explaining this... the oneness to allness of you for explaining this. Do you have advice for Natalie and anyone else that she might share this with? Do you have advice of how to enjoy the journey?

There's a lot of people who get caught up in the density, the duality, the extremes of duality for sometimes an entire lifetime, and there's a lot of this still existing in the world. Is there a message that can help people who are attempting to move themselves within their own experience into the ease and the effortlessness, and the fun and the joy, and the congruency and alignment with the more lighter aspects of the human expression while still honoring the shadow? Is there any advice that you have for them? Do you have advice or guidance on how to elevate out of that density?

N: I'm seeing money as this dark energy. It's not dark as in negative or positive, but heavy, we'll say. It's money that keeps the soul from flying free and being playful with the energies.

There needs to be a new perspective on money. That's the common fear among the collective, and especially people who Natalie serves and her audience. They want to believe—and energetically they feel—themselves to be on that higher plane, but the money aspect is what gets them stuck and sticky in the density.

B: And how can we move ourselves out of it and keep uplifting them? I experience that sometimes too, right? Up and down, ebb and flow. So, how can we, as wayshowers, really embody that sticky-free frequency with our financial abundance and reciprocity?

My [spirit] team always says money is just a frequency that exists within all of us, that we've collectively agreed upon experiencing in this particular way that we have for so long. But they're also encouraging us to shift more into 5D views and above of money—of the frequency to shift that duality—to deflate some of that stickiness. So, do they have advice on this, on how we do this?

N: Whoa, there's so much. Okay, let's see.

B: Can you guys bring it in slower?

N: Money, like you were saying, is a collective frequency. Currency is a conduit for the energies that are put into it. And the mass majority of people in the world are putting in negative energy. Not negative as in bad, but just dense.

B: Heavy. Slower.

N: Yeah, and I just see tearing open the illusion. I see what would happen if we didn't have any money. The illusions that come up when we ask ourselves that question are not real. We picture homelessness, bills not getting paid... whatever. I don't want to bring that [energy] in, but we all know it's easy to step into the mindset of thinking about where that road would go. But that's a completely false illusion of what would actually happen.

And I'm... Whoa. This is a big energy.

Trading. Trading. Normalize trading.

B: Is that why so many of my friends recently have asked me to trade? It's pretty wild. I've had three of my friends in the last two weeks ask me to do trades.

N: Yeah, it's the wave of the future.

The human part of me is like, "What the hell!" But the spirit parts are like, "In the future, there will not be any money."

B: I believe that my team showed me that, too. We won't need it!

N: Exactly. And we see that as like, "Oh no!" But actually it's the most beautiful opening that could ever possibly occur. And we need to see it as a beautiful opening.

So, Natalie has to lead the way through trading, and that scares her. Even bringing this across, she's like, "What the hell?"

B: I understand.

N: And it's not fully anchored yet... is also part of it. But I do see myself as a role model, and that's very important to me... to embody the energies that I teach and share. That's why I've been feeling really strange lately with my work. I feel like I'm like, "Oh, business astrology," but I don't use business astrology anymore. I'm peering back into myself seven years ago in order to teach that.

Now, I see myself holding this ball of light and I'm like, "I don't know what I've got here, but I have to have this ball of light. I'm going to *live* this ball of light! And I don't know exactly what it is, but it's light and that's important. So, we're just going to *accept* trading... Okay, I don't know what's going to happen, but this is what I'm doing."

B: Absolutely.

N: And that's so funny because yesterday I was supposed to be doing something else, but I decided I'm going to build my entire website for hypnosis sessions from start to finish. I literally built the whole website, and it's beautiful. And then the very last thing was to put a price. And I'm like, "No, I'm not going to put a price. We'll just wait on that. I'm feeling some weird energy around that. I'm just not going to put one yet."

B: And let Higher Self say why Natalie felt like saying "no" to the price.

N: There's so much density in money. It needs to be disconnected from. It's okay to charge for the courses and things I've already made. It's okay to charge a lot of money for those things because the people who are going into those containers operate on that frequency. So, that makes sense to them. They actually want to pay that price because it feels congruent with them and their current state. But quantum hypnosis is different. It is not to be charged for initially. Mic drop!

Note: All of the sessions in this book were conducted through trades. However, I still accept money if someone feels they do not know what to trade.

B: I mean, I charge for mine.

N: You do. But for Natalie, at least at this current moment, it's not always appropriate, because part of it is we want her to tune into the energy of the person who is requesting and ask herself, "Does that feel like a service she wants to provide for that person?"

Because a lot of this quantum healing... it does kind of fit into the category of "work" for her. She is beyond a job, a career, and she keeps trying to put herself in—pigeonhole herself in—these areas. And we just don't want that energy anymore. (Deep sigh)

And I feel like, yeah, not always charging for it... it just keeps a really crystal clear intention of tuning in. Like, do I have energy for this?

This may not be your experience with your work that you (Bridget) do, but I don't need another empire! I'm constantly trying to build empires and we're done with that. This is really meant to be a healing service. And at the root of it is really me learning about the universe through other vessels. And, of course, they're getting a lot out of it as well. And there is an element of service to it that is integral.

B: Yes. Beautiful.

Okay, so I would love to ask, "Question 2: Higher Self, can you tell Natalie about her pre-birth plan for this life that she's in?" I feel like we touched on this earlier, but can you bring anything else in for this?

N: To get into the specifics would be denying the totality—the energetic totality of it—because that's a different level. That's actually a lower level than she's currently communicating from because it ties in her past lives and karma and stuff like that. And this [current energy she's channeling] is so much bigger than all that.

So, really the plan is to have fun and to anchor [light]. I mean, isn't this *everybody's* purpose on some level? To anchor the high dimensional frequencies of the pink and the teal and the luminescent white [the higher frequencies of our souls]. It's not even purple I see. It's like the purple is on the edges of the white. It's interesting. It always comes back to color, but that's what it is.

And I have this very visceral feeling of drilling into the Earth and pouring sparkly bits into the concrete. And that's what the real true purpose is at the higher level. And really building a stairwell. The stairwell starts at the bottom as concrete, and then it turns into the material of those ghost chairs—you know those clear chairs everybody has at their wedding? (Both laugh)

It just turns into that. And then it's vaporizing away at the top.

B: Beautiful.

N: And it's all for fun. It's not serious. It's not like, "Oh, we have to save their souls or they'll be doomed!" It's none of that. It's so hilarious! We're laughing so hard about that.

B: It's about us remembering who we are and playing while we do it, right?

N: And even the fear-based stories. They're so cute. We just think it's adorable. You guys are really cute.

B: Okay, so, "Question 3: Her guides are always saying to her, "Color her wonderful." I feel like this has been explained multiple times today, but are there any other insights or depth of information that you would like to express to Natalie now about "color me wonderful" and the hybrid energy that she described earlier? Would you like to add anything to that?

N: [Combining all of the energies] is a practice, because at first I saw—when you swim in the ocean–sometimes there's a warm area and a cool area if there is an underwater spring. It's not all the same temperature even if it's the same body of water. And it's like you can swim in between energy states, but the process of fully integrating is a practice.

So, I just did it right now, energetically, laying here as you were speaking. It's something I have to practice. I have to practice pulling [the integrated energy of the Higher Self] into my core, but it's all there and it's really easy. It's not hard to do by any means. It's just an intention and it's kind of like homework to practice that.

I hate the word "work". The word "work" just came back in! (Laughs)

B: I like to call it sacred practice.

N: It's just something to play with, we'll say. Something to do. And it will become natural. You won't even have to think about it after a while.

But we don't want to just say, "Zap! It's all integrated as of today," because we don't want to take away the experience of you integrating them within yourself... "you" being Natalie and whoever, whomever.

B: Beautiful. That's fine. It's always whatever is in Natalie's highest and best. We know my intention is so that whatever can be initiated in the now, and moved forward in, we do. But, of course, if that's not in alignment—if it's not congruent with the joy and the pleasure of the expression—then, of course, we're not asking to subvert what is right.

N: And it's very easy. It's like when you're learning how to drive. Your parent doesn't turn the key in the ignition for you. You do it yourself, and it's so easy to turn the ignition.

B: So, can we show her... let's do it one more time. Let's bring it in. Very focused... practice pulling into the core and let it be obvious and easy so that she can always return to this in her waking reality and beyond, whenever it's aligned and joyful and happy and all the things.

N: She's moving past mixing colors on the page into mixing colors within her. It's so easy to do. It really is. But I noticed there's a block in my back.

B: Yes. So, let's take the block, the perceived blockage, and let's go ahead... if there's anything important about it, let's go ahead and bring it to the light and explain it. And if not, let's go ahead and dissolve it, transmute it, whatever feels aligned.

N: A spirit just flew out of my back. They're just past life selves clinging on.

Bridget spends a few moments doing an energy clearing to release any blocked energies.

N: [Natalie]'s trying to allow the full healing to take place in this moment. Yet some of the activities we presented will further assist, like the trading for example, that will really be... I almost want to be like—this is a really funny way to say it—but it's like, "Screw you, past selves. We don't need this [fear-based money] bullshit."

B: But with love...

N: Yeah, with total love! It's hilarious. It's like I'm joking as I'm flicking them off, and just fully... just completely... detaching from that [fear-based scarcity] energy around money.

B: But there's also lots of pathways. Natalie has lots of pathways to support herself financially in what we will call the transition period, right?

N: Yes. And this isn't to say you're only trading for everything. It's just offering the opportunity for that particular service. I've created many things in the past that still give recurring revenue or whatever, and that's fine.

But trading, and that's a really important keyword here… because I see her already going into like, "Oh my God, I'm going to have to work for free?!" No, no, no. Trade. Trade!

B: There has to be an exchange.

N: They have to have something of value for you. This can't be a free service.

B: It's an energy exchange.

N: Yes. It's "Do you have something that could assist me?" It could be really small, it could be a testimonial, it could be feedback, it could be… maybe they do Reiki or something. If that feels like what you desire at that moment, then it's fine. It doesn't have to be like, "Okay, this should be this much, so you have to give me this much of whatever. "

And this is a practice, too. We're not saying it's a way of life. We're not saying you're a monk or a nun or something [sacrificing up everything you have to be of service]. It's an exercise of allowing the frequencies to come in that are of much higher value than financial currency.

B: Beautiful. Is there anything that we might not have thought to ask that is appropriate to either bring in for her or to express currently?

N: I'm just feeling all the anxieties of the human self. The social anxiety. "What will people think? Do I look okay?"

I don't really know how to describe that because humans just live it. They don't question it, really. I just feel like we could cleanse that.

Bridget spends a few minutes doing an energy clearing to remove the energy of social anxiety from both my Higher Self's energy field and the collective energy field.

N: Whoa, that's amazing. (Giggles)

I saw that our light body is what makes us beautiful. Hair, makeup, whatever... none of that matters when you're vibrating in alignment with your light body frequency, and that's what makes someone beautiful when we see the spark in them.

And then I saw my face in all my past lifetimes, all on top of each other. I was an energy swimming through it all and out of it, and there was a healing waterfall flowing down over it all.

After the waterfall, I saw myself as Pleiadian/Arcturian combined inside of myself almost like ET. I'm meant to just see myself as that instead, and operate my life as all of these beings [that I am] when I carry myself in the world. It's just my Higher Self, really. But it's funny to me, it helps me to think of it as ET or something... like an actual creature. Then, it's like I'm here doing experiments. I'm not so attached to the human layer.

It's like when you put on pajamas to go to sleep, those aren't the normal clothes you wear all day. That's kind of what Natalie is in a way. You're putting on a set of clothes [or a human identity and personality] to do a certain task for a temporary amount of time. And I don't need to identify with it so strongly because a lot of that stems from being in lower densities. It's fear that calls your attention to those things on the physical plane that create judgment—and society, of course, echoes it out—but we only buy into the fear of being different or not fitting in when we're not tuning into our light body frequency.

So, that's the way it comes back to that... "playful exercise" (avoiding the word "homework") of calling all the colors of our energy in.

B: Is there anything else that would like to come through? Do we feel complete, Higher Self and soul team collective, in today's journey?

N: Yes. We are complete.

ADDITIONAL RESOURCES

If you are interested in getting a hypnosis session to connect with your Higher Self, please visit **www.higherselfsessions.co**

Get trained to become a Quantum Healing Hypnosis Technique (QHHT®) Practitioner yourself at **www.qhhtofficial.com**

If you would like to learn more about the subjects in this book, the following are recommended reads by other authors:

- *Between Death and Life* by Dolores Cannon
- *The Hidden Search for Sacred Knowledge* by Dolores Cannon
- *Horns of the Goddess* by Dolores Cannon
- *The Three Waves of Volunteers* by Dolores Cannon
- *Your Soul's Gift: The Healing Power of the Life You Planned Before You Were Born* by Robert Schwartz
- *Your Soul's Plan: Discovering the Real Meaning of the Life You Planned Before You Were Born* by Robert Schwartz
- *Many Lives, Many Masters* by Brian Weiss
- *Same Soul, Many Bodies* by Brian Weiss

- *Journey of Souls* by Michael Newton
- *Destiny of Souls* by Michael Newton
- *Wisdom of Souls* by Michael Newton
- *Akashic Records: Case Studies of Past Lives* by Lois J. Wetzel
- *Reincarnation: Past Lives and the Akashic Record* by Lois J. Wetzel
- *From Deep Space with Love: A Conversation about Consciousness, the Universe, and Building a Better World* by Mike Dooley with Tracy Farquar
- *Bringers of the Dawn: Teachings from the Pleiadians* by Barbara Marciniak
- *Conversations with Laarkmaa: A Pleiadian View of the New Reality* by Cullen Baird Smith and Pia Orleane
- *Songs of the Arcturians and The Arcturian Star Chronicles (Volumes 1-4)* by Patricia Pereira
- *The Sophia Code: A Living Transmission from the Sophia Dragon Tribe* by Kaia Ra
- *Initiation* by Elisabeth Haich
- *Angels in My Hair: The True Story of a Modern-Day Irish Mystic* by Lorna Byrne
- *The New Angel Messages: Awaken with the Angels* by Shunanda Scott

ACKNOWLEDGMENTS

Thank you to the late Dolores Cannon and her daughter Julia Cannon for developing the methods that were used to find the information in this book and for providing the training that was necessary for me to interview the Higher Self.

A huge thank you to all of the clients who were a part of this book for vulnerably sharing your sessions with the world. I know it is not easy to be so open about your earthside learnings, but your Higher Self's messages have now gone on to inspire many. Thank you also to all of the clients whose sessions were not included in this book for the inspiration and practice—you matter and you are important, too.

So much gratitude to Valerie deBeaumont (**www.valeriedebeaumont.com**) and Bridget Renee Holliday (**www.bridgetreneeholliday.com**) for holding space for me in my hypnosis sessions and being powerful role models for me to look up to as I embarked on this journey.

Thank you to my beta reader team, especially Kailanianna Ablog, Lisa McConnell, Whibs Howes, Deborah Heltzer, Brad Gray, Bianca Aponte, Melissa Williams, and Jann Henkes for sharing your thoughtful feedback and for helping this book make more sense to a wider audience.

Thank you to my past life self, who had a near-death experience where he discovered that we have spirit guides watching over us. He tried to share this information with others, but was not believed or listened to. This book is for you/me/us, a symbol of breaking free of societal opinions and expectations and honoring my truth even if it freaks people out.

ABOUT THE AUTHOR

Natalie Walstein is a multi-passionate spiritual seeker, astrologer, and Pisces Sun & Moon with Sagittarius Rising. As a quantum hypnosis practitioner, she uses her voice to heal and soothe her clients into a dreamlike trance state to find their own answers through channeling their Higher Selves.

As the founder of Divine Flow Publishing Co., Natalie's calling is to elevate the vibration of the planet with new age books that help to establish more uplifting belief systems so we can trust the universe, love ourselves more, and become a more loving human community on Earth. She was born and raised in Minneapolis, Minnesota, but currently resides in her "heart home" on the island of Maui in Hawaii with her dog, Flower.

Also by this Author:

- *Find Your Cosmic Calling: A Guide to Discovering Your Life's Work with Astrology* (English, 2022)
- *AstroRêve: Un guide pour découvrir votre mission de vie avec l'astrologie* (French, 2023)
- *Scritto nelle stelle: Una guida per scoprire la tua vocazione con l'astrologia* (Italian, 2024)

www.ingramcontent.com/pod-product-compliance
Lightning Source LLC
Chambersburg PA
CBHW050523100526
44581CB00002B/85